T0321125

The Greatest American Football Story that has Never Been Told

The Greatest American Football Story that has Never Been Told

How Gridiron Stopped the War

Anthony Wootton

First published by Pitch Publishing, 2024

Pitch Publishing
9 Donnington Park,
85 Birdham Road,
Chichester,
West Sussex,
PO20 7AJ
www.pitchpublishing.co.uk
info@pitchpublishing.co.uk

A CIP catalogue record is available for this book from the British Library.

ISBN 978 1 80150 677 9

Typesetting and origination by Pitch Publishing

Printed and bound in Great Britain by TJ Books, Padstow

Contents

For Julia, my fabulous cheerleader whose patience is limitless.

To Louis and Ben, my boys. Follow your dreams and amazing things will happen.

For Andrew and Kathy for all your kindness and support, you're both wonderful.

To Roy and Stan, my two grandfathers whose stories I loved to hear. You sparked my interest in the war. I miss you both.

Introduction

SPORT HAS the unique power to unite people. It has provided light even in the darkest of times. It is a source of hope, inspiration, freedom, and respite.

That first Christmas during the First World War along parts of the Western Front in 1914, British and German soldiers called a truce and played a game of football. The trained instinct to protect and kill that had been instilled into them, and the unexpected horrors of the previous five months, were put aside, and spirits were, all too briefly, raised by the kick of a ball. They were unified by the international language of sport.

I discovered the story of the Tea Bowl while I was researching American football games that had been played in southern England generations later. I had interviewed Steve Rains, former coach of the British amateur team, the Farnham Knights, about his career and how he became involved in the sport.

Rains remembered the days he spent watching games from the bleachers inside the US Air Force base at Greenham Common near Newbury, Berkshire. Greenham had a long history with US forces, dating back to the Second World War. It was the location where General Dwight D. Eisenhower, Commander-in-Chief of the Allied Expeditionary Force, addressed paratroopers from the 101st Airborne on the eve of D-Day.

Throughout the 1980s it was the base for the USAF's nuclear cruise missiles. Although for Rains, it was a piece of America where cars drove on the other side of the road and people paid for things in dollars. Within the compound was a gridiron, a field, and lines where servicemen could switch off from the threat of war and play a sport that they loved. They were thousands of miles from home, but sport was their family, providing comfort in the most testing of times.

The NFL has grown massively in the United Kingdom in the 21st century. Ever since the Miami Dolphins hosted a regular season game against the New York Giants at Wembley Stadium on October 28, 2007, London has become an important market for the league.

Multiple games are played each year in the UK capital, selling out 61,000 and 85,000 seats at Tottenham and Wembley, respectively.

Long before this had become a possibility, decades before the NFL merger brought us the Super Bowl, two football games were played inside a major London stadium. Each was a bowl game, and they attracted crowds of more than 30,000 and 50,000 spectators. They were the Tea and Coffee Bowls.

What was striking about these games was not the size of the crowds, tens of thousands of people watching a peculiar form of rugby in west London, but the number of professional players who were involved: CFL and NFL stars of their day who had paused their careers to risk their lives so that they could protect their countries. These were not just squad players either. All-star running backs and quarterbacks featured, some of whom had only seen their loved ones once since enlisting. Many of whom had seen comrades die.

These players would eventually be reunited with family; others, tragically, paid the ultimate sacrifice.

The games happened thanks to a chance encounter in a London pub over the Christmas of 1943. A Canadian officer became engaged in conversation about sport with an American. The chat was about American football and, several drinks later, plans were in place to put on a game. But it would not be any game. This was not to be seven versus seven in the nearby park. It would be a game that featured the best players each side had to offer. It would be so big that troops were to be granted leave from active service to train.

It would be a simple game that would bring light in the darkest of times.

The Greatest American Football Story Is Never Been Told is about those games at White City Stadium in London on February 13 and March 19, 1944. Canada vs. USA. Some of the best players the CFL had to offer and title-winning quarterbacks from the NFL. Hall of Fame players along with names so good there are modern-day awards that are presented in their honour.

The book features full match reports from those games in 1944 and shares memories from a few of the players involved. Memories that have not publicly been shared before. We gain insight into the lives of some of those football stars and, sadly, the tragic loss of the men who were killed in action.

This book also looks at the NFL's ongoing commitment to honouring the armed forces and how those service personnel have helped grow the sport of American football around the world. We delve into the special relationship the forces and National Football League have and explore the nuances between the two.

As the NFL continues to grow internationally, with games played in London and Germany, I look back at the League's early attempts at expansion with the World League of American Football in the early 1990s. The people responsible for developing NFL Europe explain how their first experiences with football (soccer) hooliganism in Germany helped lay the foundations of the impressive fan base we see in the country today: a. fan base that has brought back-to-back regular season games to the city of Frankfurt. It is also a fan base that gave the legendary Tom Brady one of his happiest football memories.

Unfortunately, with war comes the tragic loss of life. Whereas fighting was not optional for the men who served during the Second World War, all of whom had other jobs to support their football careers, the Arizona Cardinals star, Pat Tillman, did have a choice. He was at the peak of his powers with multi-million-dollar contract offers on the table. Following the attack on his country in 2001, the young man felt a sense of duty to serve. Pat's coach from that Cardinals team recalls their conversations and the terrible news of his death whilst on duty in Afghanistan.

The tragedy of Pat Tillman's story sent shockwaves around the world.

American football truly went international in the 1940s. Decades later, the growth of the sport has been beyond the wildest dreams of those young men who took part. Boundaries have been broken and communities forged around the world through the sport they loved so dearly that it gave them solace at a time when war had cast a shadow over their lives like a winter fog clouding out the joyful embrace of the sun.

The power of sport can never be underestimated.

SECTION 1:

Football Stars Far from Home

CHAPTER 1

The Toll of War

'The overwhelming majority of our people have met the demands of this war with magnificent courage and understanding. They have accepted inconveniences; they have accepted hardships; they have accepted tragic sacrifices.'

– President Franklin D. Roosevelt

MOST CANADIANS had been in Britain since 1940. The country declared war on Germany soon after Britain had in September 1939. Many Canadians initially headed to the Hampshire military town of Aldershot. Resident Aldershot divisions had been immediately mobilised and moved out at the outbreak of both world wars, so the camp was vacant.

The Canadians started arriving in December 1939, and large numbers headed over late into 1940. Although, as the Canadian Army grew and the headquarters moved out of Aldershot, the town itself remained the centre for the Army as they arrived in Britain. Thousands upon thousands of Canucks passed through that tiny part of Hampshire.

Initially, they were very unhappy, especially those that arrived in the December of '39. It was a particularly bad winter, and they were completely unprepared for it. Even though the Canadians were used to the cold, they were not accustomed to the cold and damp of English winters. Nor were they used to the conditions of their barracks, which were large rooms of 15 or 20 men. The only source of heat they received came from a single iron stove, which was hopelessly inadequate. They had not even tasted war, but life had already become unbearable. According to Paul Vickers, local historian, and chairman of The Friends of Aldershot Military Museum, many of the Canadians wondered what they'd come into.

'They did get a warm welcome from the local population,' Vickers said. 'And there is a lovely story of one of the local residents from Christmas 1939, who was taking pity on the Canadians. He drove his car around North Camp, picked up a couple of Canadian soldiers who were walking to the nearest pub and invited them to his home and gave them Christmas dinner.

'That is typical of the sort of relationship that developed between the Canadians and the local population here in Aldershot,' added Vickers, 'and it started again with the Americans when they started to arrive a few years later.'

Early in the Second World War the Canadians had trained hard in the Hampshire countryside and had got themselves ready for combat. Therefore, when the Dieppe raid was launched in the summer of 1942, most of the men who were sent there had been drawn from the Canadians based in Aldershot. Of the 6,000 men that took part in the raid, nearly 5,000 of them were Canadians.

The raid, Operation Jubilee, was a disaster. Dieppe had the highest number of Canadian casualties in a single day during World Watr II, with 907 killed, 586 wounded, and 1,874 taken prisoner. There were 237 ships and landing craft in the Dieppe flotilla, and some accounts reported that the weapons that troops saw on the ships had never been fired.

RAF bombers were meant to hit the town the night before; however, they failed to do their job. Dieppe is a coastal town with white cliffs and stone beaches. Being able to run on stones is a lot more difficult than running on sand. The soldiers were forced to carry the weight of military equipment and had no chance of dragging artillery across the beach. They were sitting ducks.

There was just one officer who returned from the beaches unwounded. He was Captain Denis Whitaker, the main protagonist of this story, who we will learn more about.

The survivors of Dieppe returned to Aldershot. Their sacrifices were not in vain, and many historians believe that the lessons learned from Dieppe were subsequently applied to the D-Day landings. The success of D-Day owed a lot to Operation Jubilee.

There were 50 American Rangers involved at Dieppe. The raid had been the first US involvement in ground combat in Europe. Only 15 Rangers landed on the beaches. Three were killed, three captured and five were wounded.

The first of more than 1.5 million American troops arrived in Britain on January 26, 1942. The US War Department had provided the young men with a guide to living abroad. Many of them had never been outside the States before, so they were given a booklet called *Instructions for American Servicemen in Britain 1942*.

The 42-page book had tips and advice such as, 'The British of all classes are enthusiastic about sports, both as amateurs and as spectators of professional sports … the great "spectator" sports are football in the autumn and winter and cricket in the spring and summer. See a "match" in either of these sports whenever you get a chance. You will get a kick out of it – if only for the difference from American sports.'

Other advice included, 'Do not make fun of British speech or accents. You sound just as funny to them, but they will be too polite to show it.'

Servicemen knew something was building at the beginning of 1944. The previous year had seen Allied forces invade Sicily and the eventual downfall of fascist power in Italy. Benito Mussolini had been arrested on July 25, 1943. Hitler poured German troops into the country to prevent any chance of a peace settlement that would take Italy out of the war.

The main allied invasion of Italy began in September. By October 1 British troops had entered Naples. Deadly battles raged on throughout the country.

Months earlier, on May 16, the infamous Dambusters raid took place. Nineteen Lancaster bombers set off on one of the most courageous and innovative operations of the Second World War. Their operation was to blow up three dams in Germany's industrial heartland. The targets were heavily protected, and the bombers had to fly as low as 60 feet, at a ground speed of 232mph, for their bouncing bombs to be effective. The problem with flying so low was that they could not pass those defences unnoticed. Of the 133 men in the aircrew who were involved in Operation Chastise, 53 were killed.

On the Eastern Front, the Soviet Union defeated the German forces at Stalingrad in February 1943. Lasting almost six months, it is one of the deadliest battles in history, which resulted in 633,000 deaths. Throughout 1943, Soviet forces were winning back towns and areas of Russia that had been taken over by Germany.

Meanwhile, Britain was plunged into darkness. It was another winter of rationing, blackouts, and bombing. Dwight D. Eisenhower arrived in January 1944 to set up the Supreme Headquarters, Allied Expeditionary Force

(SHAEF). Plans for a cross-Channel assault by Allied forces were developing.

Throughout the Second World War, more than two million American servicemen passed through Britain. The height of activity was in 1944 when the country housed nearly half a million men stationed with the United States Army Air Forces. Around 200 airfields had been built, each housing 2,500 men. Small towns and villages were taken over by Americans, converting halls and properties into headquarters.

So, by Christmas of 1943, there was a sense of anxiousness around Canadian and American troops in Great Britain. Something was happening, preparations had begun, but they did not know exactly what it was or when it would be.

For many Canadian troops it was another cold and dull English winter, thousands of miles from the comfort of family and home. This winter had taken a toll on them because, combined with the miserable cold English climate, they were pressured with the intensive training for what would eventually become the invasion of France. The devastating assault on the northern coastline of Europe at Dieppe was still clear in their minds.

Having spent days in the countryside, shivering in damp tents and taking precautions against live ammunition in his combat manoeuvres, a Canadian major took himself into the warm confines of a London pub while on weekend leave.

In 1996 Denis and his wife, Shelagh Whitaker, were recording his memories of the Tea Bowl. It was clear that the games against the Americans were very fond memories for him. About that visit to the London pub, he told Shelagh, 'I started talking to a fellow next to me, who turned out to be a lieutenant in the American Army Recreational Services. He mentioned that he was pretty interested in football and had just brought over six complete sets of equipment for football teams.'

This got Whitaker excited. Whether or not it was the beer flowing inside of him, the MVP QB had an idea. 'I knew a number of Canadians serving in Britain who had played pro or college football, so several beers later I found myself talking this fellow into lending us some uniforms and putting together a USA vs. Canada match.'

And so, the idea for the Tea Bowl was born.

CHAPTER 2

Denis Whitaker: A Warrior that was Great

'I imagine a lot of those soldiers who saw the game kept memories too, that might have helped keep them sane in the months to come.'

– Denis Whitaker

NONE OF the events that occurred at White City Stadium in this story would have happened without Denis Whitaker. Whitaker was a unicorn. He was a natural born leader, visionary, and winner. He was an inspiration to many.

When he died on May 30, 2001, the *New York Times* ran an obituary with the headline, 'Denis Whitaker, 86, Highly Decorated Canadian War Hero'. The obit then opened with, 'Brigadier-General Denis Whitaker, one of Canada's most highly decorated army officers of World War Two and a military historian and sportsman, died May 30 in Oakville, Ontario. He was 86.' Denis lived a life less ordinary. He had excelled at everything he did.

There are many stories about Denis that stick with me, none more so than the Tea Bowl. However, another memorable tale was shared by his daughter, Gail Whitaker Thompson, when I first met her in June 2017. We sat in an Italian restaurant in St John's Wood, London.

Denis and his firsty wife, Nita, had thrown a party at his farm in Canada when there was a knock at the door. (Dennis and Nita had been married for over 30 years before he married Shelasg in 1973.) A native Canadian chief wanted to speak with him and asked for Hoddreyus Go Wa. That was the name given to Whitaker when he was made an honorary chief of the local Onondaga tribe. The name means 'A Warrior that was Great'. The two men left the party and Whitaker gave the chief his time to help him with what he needed doing.

Gail was very proud of sharing that story with me. Her father had members of the Onondaga tribe in his regiment during the Second World War. The honour given to Whitaker was their way of saying thanks for ensuring their men returned home safely. Despite being young himself, Whitaker was responsible for ensuring the safety of countless others during the war. It appears that Denis Whitaker was a warrior that was destined for great things from the moment he was born.

Throughout his remarkable life he met royalty, world leaders and sporting greats. Whilst on tour in England, Whitaker took King George VI for his first ride in a Bren Gun Carrier and later became familiar with the king's son-in-law, Prince Philip. The Duke of Edinburgh had become acquainted with Denis during Whitaker's time as chair of the Canadian equestrian team. The duke was president of the International Federation for Equestrian Sports.

Denis's father was Major Guy Whitaker. Guy was posted overseas during the First World War and returned to Canada as a lieutenant. Denis was the first born and grew up as a successful athlete.

Denis Whitaker, also a top academic, attended the University of Toronto, and then the Royal Military College of Canada (RMC) at Kingston, Ontario. While at RMC he had been captain of the football team in 1936–37. Following graduation, he was signed as a quarterback by the Canadian

Football League (CFL) team, the Hamilton Tigers. In 1938 Whitaker was nominated the All-Eastern quarterback, which was the most valuable QB of his conference.

When Britain declared war on Germany in 1939, 'Denny' had been commissioned to the Royal Hamilton Light Infantry (RHLI) and was told to await orders to be sent overseas. Seven days later, Canada also declared war on the Germans, which meant his call-up would come at any moment.

Whitaker was called into action in June 1940, just as training had begun for the new Canadian football season. Whitaker sailed off to England, leaving behind his pregnant wife and a blossoming professional sports career.

By the time Denis Whitaker entered that London pub at Christmastime in 1943, he had witnessed first-hand the tremendous loss of life at the disastrous Dieppe raid and had only seen his infant daughter, Gail, once. She was two when he got to meet her for the first time in 1942. It came during short leave that had been granted to him after Dieppe.

Whitaker had also been injured in 1943. He and his battalion were in northern France where they sustained three days and nights of heavy fire. Whitaker had finally lain down in his cot under a makeshift cover that was dug in a trench when a shell landed and exploded near his face.

Denny was knocked unconscious and hospitalised because of his wounds. But in true Denny style, he was back with his regiment as soon as clearance was granted. He was a man who had been gifted with natural leadership; a unique trait that allowed him to excel at everything he did. Peter Young, the friend and companion he had made at the Royal Hamilton Light Infantry in later life, said Whitaker's experience as a quarterback helped him command soldiers on the battlefield, just as he led his offence on the gridiron.

'It is my belief that because he played football as a quarterback, he had to lead [in the Army],' said Young. Peter Young joined the RHLI in 1962; he was 16. By the 1980s he had been promoted to the position of commander. It was during his time as the senior ranking officer that Young got to know Whitaker more personally.

'Those professional players [who served during World War II] were never going to follow someone because they were told to,' Peter said. 'You have to show your leadership as a quarterback. And I think that those traits transferred, maybe back and forth. 'I use that as an example of a quarterback, "follow me, you must do that. Here's what we're going to do, I've got this."'

Peter has been a military leader. He has seen leadership done well and has also seen it done badly. He knows the traits that an individual requires to engage, inspire, and motivate a group of people.

'I think those quarterback attributes transposed to the military in a different way. You are only going to get knocked down on a football field [as opposed to a battlefield],' Peter added.

'But that's what I use when talking about leadership in my job. It's the lead by example. Obviously, you have established some credentials in your day-to-day work as a signal caller.'

The great quarterbacks have the unique ability to lead their teams on game-winning drives when the odds are stacked against them. Whether it's Joe Montana in Super Bowl XXIII or Tom Brady from 28-3 down to the Atlanta Falcons. With trenches crumbling, blitzes raining down on them, they have an instinct to read their battlefield, unlock opponents and inspire team-mates to maximise the talent at their disposal.

'There are natural leaders, and some have to work at it, but it all works out the same, that people will follow you when you ask them to.'

Denny did not have to return to his regiment after his injury in 1943, but he wanted to. He felt it was his responsibility to his men that he was there for them as their leader.

As Peter Young put it, 'To be wounded and then jump back into combat, as so many people did, is just beyond me.'

There was a sense of patriotism and camaraderie to complete the job. Denis Whitaker was responsible for a group of young men, many of whom were barely 20 years old and alone in a country that was totally alien to them and thousands of miles from home. Most of those men had never been outside of their Canadian provinces before.

They were so far from the confines and sanctuary of the things they were used to, an ocean apart from friends, family, and loved ones. The only companionship that these twenty-somethings had was with each other. Despite only being 28 years old himself, Denny was the paternal figure. He was the man they looked to in times of crisis. On the battlefield, Denis Whitaker was the signal caller, working his offensive units on the front line. He knew his role and he executed his routes to win and, more importantly, ensure the safety of his regiment.

At Dieppe, two-thirds of Denis's battalion had been killed or captured. As for the third that made it out, half of them were wounded. Denny was the most senior ranking officer that made it back unscathed, and he was a junior captain at the time.

The task he had been given was to reach the church in the town, so that they could set up battalion headquarters and fortify it with defences.

However, the Germans were waiting. Positioned at the top of the beach and with vantage points from the nearby clifftops, they had the upper hand over the 6,000 Allied troops who were landing on the shoreline.

'I've been to Dieppe so many times now,' said Peter Young, 'and you just look at the beach, with the stones, there's no sand, and the fortifications, and I just shake my head.'

Before the war, Dieppe had been a tourist destination for British holidaymakers. Those white cliffs and pebble beaches would have been very familiar to the British surveillance teams. The Dieppe raid became Canada's most disastrous military failure of the war. How could they be so underprepared? The reasons for the raid and its defeat remain hotly debated issues today.

The Canadians trained for it along the Dorset coastline, which resembled the Dieppe area. There was a mock exercise that did not go well. Units landed miles off target and the tank landing craft arrived an hour late. Improvements were made during later training exercises, leaving officers satisfied that the raid would work. It did not.

Speaking with the Canadian press in 2017, Honorary Colonel David Lloyd Hart recalled his experience of the Dieppe raid. Hart was a communications officer who had been stuck on a crippled boat 15 feet from shore. He was unable to swim for the beach because he could not leave the vessel's radio unit. 'The fire was terrible,' he said in the interview.

'There was mortar fire, and there were machine-gun nests in the cliffs which weren't seen by our intelligence people because they had them covered, and they had heavy six-pounder or more cannons shooting at us. We were sitting ducks.'

Not only had soldiers been sent into a port that was so heavily guarded, but they were also ordered to continue to attack while disaster had struck and thousands lay on the beach, either wounded or dead. The English Channel turned red with the blood. Those who had been taken prisoner were shipped to camps in boxcars alongside horses.

'One year I went down right to the water's edge just before daylight to commemorate with one of the other Canadian regiments,' Young recalled. 'Then we had to climb back up [to the promenade] and I was wearing comfortable and very practical hiking shoes. There was a part where we had to help each other up, so imagine being in leather boots with horseshoe cleats on the soles with all of your gear on.'

It would have been like running through treacle with bullets flying past you from every angle and shells exploding in all directions.

'I get chills every time I go there,' Young said, 'or even now thinking about it.

'I don't know how people like Denny got out; you hope that you'd do the same thing. But when you really think about it, how he got not only himself out, but motivated his men to do what they did, is a mark of the man's leadership.'

Whitaker knew it was impossible to get all his men off the beach, but he saw a casino and led them towards it. They cut through the wire entanglements that blocked the entrance and ran in, firing their guns. The building was filled with Germans, many of whom raised their hands in surrender.

Denny's daughter, Gail, told me that he and a few others jumped out of a window under heavy fire and hid in a wooden shelter. That shelter turned out to be a latrine. For more than half an hour they laid in German excrement, hidden from enemy fire.

Aware that there was no commanding officer in sight, Whitaker led his men back to the casino, dodging fire as they ran. They held there until orders to evacuate came. Under a smokescreen, Denny and his regiment headed for the landing craft and returned to England.

'The story goes,' Peter Young told me, 'his batman [orderly] woke him up in England. And of course, Denny was dead asleep in the morning after they got back. The batman says that Denny must go and give an account of what happened to Admiral [Louis] Mountbatten at a debrief in London. And of course, Denny thought this was a joke and said some rude things to his batman, even though it was true.'

With young men dying around him in unthinkable numbers, the quarterback had managed to stick to his objective. However, he was quick to point out that he was not the only hero that day, explaining that thousands of others had been equally gallant. According to Young, Denny did not hold back when sharing his thoughts on the shambolic planning that had cost so many people their lives. There was no shying away from holding those senior figures accountable.

For his heroics on that disastrous day, Denis Whitaker was awarded the Distinguished Service Order. It was an honour that was ordered by the United Kingdom and the Commonwealth for 'distinguished services during active operations against the enemy'.

Denis Whitaker was not involved in the Normandy landings on D-Day. It was decided that his regiment should join the invasion six days later. Towards the end of the war, Whitaker, as commander of the RHLI, was instrumental in Operation Veritable, which formed part of the Battle of the Rhineland. It is regarded as the battle that finally won the war.

Denis and his men led with heavy artillery, including tanks, and had advanced successfully during daylight hours. However, that night the Germans hit back and bombarded them relentlessly with tanks and infantry. The constant barrage lasted hours, striking a huge blow to the Allied forces, who suffered multiple injuries and loss of life.

Under enormous pressure, Whitaker set up a counter attack of his own, which included the destruction of two 25.2-tonne Panzer IV tanks. This strike allowed the Allies to advance and destroy other German tanks. His actions helped them to eventually take control of the area. It was the Battle of Goch-Calcar Road and his leadership earned him a second Distinguished Service Order.

According to Peter Young, Denis Whitaker ranks high among the great Canadian military leaders throughout history. 'There are so many accounts of bravery involving Canadian forces throughout that war, and others,' said Young. 'But Denny was up there with those. He showed natural leadership at times of huge pressure. Pressure you and I cannot even imagine.

'Denis Whitaker is on my shortlist of heroes.'

It comes as no surprise, therefore, that Denny's natural ability to lead sprang into action as the beer flowed in that London pub during the Christmas period of 1943.

He had the idea for a morale-boosting football game against the Yanks. He also had access to equipment. All he had to do was convince the powers that be that this alcohol-induced brainwave was something they could pull off. So, he approached Lieutenant-General Kenneth Stuart, who was Chief of Staff at the Canadian Military Headquarters.

Stuart and Whitaker had known each other from their time at RMC. The lieutenant-general was a big football fan and, unsurprisingly, was very enthusiastic about the idea. He agreed with Major Whitaker that this game would be a morale-booster for the units. Stuart pulled rank and gave the green light. The date and venue were set for February 13, 1944, at White City Stadium in west London.

'I saw many examples of that in Denny's later life where little things he did impacted so many,' remembered Peter Young. 'Even if it was just the little things, he was always solving problems. He was always trying to improve. So, there is no doubt in my mind that he was thinking about how to boost the morale of his men when this conversation took place.'

Peter explained, 'My dad was a bomber with the Royal Canadian Air Force. And we finally got a hold of a little personal diary. In it he wrote that boredom and homesickness were the big things they had to deal with in between missions. They would also have the boredom or frustration of all the training, which would have been the same, over, and over. And, of course, we know why they had to do it.'

Denny felt it; therefore, he visualised that idea, took it and, with his quarterback instincts, ran with it.

'I do not know where he could have come up with another idea that would have positively impacted so many people for a short period of time. How fantastic. It's just unbelievable,' Young said.

Whitaker was wounded twice during the war and rose to be Canada's youngest brigadier-general at the time. He was given the titles of Officer of the Legion of Honour (France), and a Commander, Order of the Crown (Belgium) as recognition for his services.

It was months after VE Day when he finally returned home to his wife and daughter. In 1946 he played again for the Hamilton Tigers. Whitaker finished his professional football career at the end of that season.

Denis's sporting exploits continued, though. From 1960 to 1982, he worked as chairman of the Canadian equestrian team, forging a relationship with the Duke of Edinburgh. Under Denny's impressive leadership, the Canadian equestrian team won gold at the 1960 Olympics in Rome, and many more medals at international tournaments.

He became a director of the Canadian Olympic Association in the 1970s and was appointed chef de mission for the Canadian team in the 1972 and 1976 Olympic Games. He also led Canada's boycott against the Moscow Games in 1980. Whitaker is credited with making show jumping an Olympic equestrian sport.

At the Royal Military College of Canada, the Whitaker Cup is awarded each year to the best team captain of an RMC varsity team.

As quarterback, commander, brigadier-general, chairman, father, and colleague, Denis Whitaker was a man people respected, admired, and looked to for inspiration. He left a legacy that has gifted the lives of more people than he could ever have imagined.

He was humble about his endeavours during the war, like so many men who fought. Denis was equally humble about his career as a professional football player. Whether it was on the battlefield, gridiron or in the boardroom, he let his actions do the talking.

Denis Whitaker is buried in Oakville, Ontario. Engraved on his headstone are the four words that describe him best: A True Canadian Hero.

CHAPTER 3

Canadian Football's Exodus

'As you wade through to the sports section of the newspapers from 1941–42 you are going past notices you'd rather not see'

– Steve Daniel, former CFL head statistician

THE CANADIAN Football League in the 1930s and 1940s was nothing like the competition it is today. Currently the league is split into two conferences, the East Division and West Division. Five teams, BC Lions, Calgary Stampeders, Edmonton Elks, and Winnipeg Blue Bombers make up the West.

The East Division includes four teams, the Hamilton Tiger-Cats, Montreal Alouettes, Ottawa Redblacks, and Toronto Argonauts. Although competition dates back to the early 1900s, the CFL wasn't formed until 1958 and the full merger of the East and West divisions did not happen until 1981.

Football has been around much longer in Canada than it has in the USA. The 2023 CFL season concluded with the 110th Grey Cup, which the Winnipeg Blue Bombers and Montreal Alouettes competed for. Montreal trailed 17-7 at half-time and sealed an epic comeback with the winning touchdown coming in the dying seconds. The Alouettes clinched their first title since 2010 with a 28-24 victory.

Canada's showpiece featured Green Day as the half-time show, while the game had the highest television audience figures for the Grey Cup since 2019 with more than 3.57 million people watching.

Well over a century before Montreal's memorable triumph, the Canadian Rugby Union (CRU) had been created in 1891. The Grey Cup trophy was commissioned by Albert Henry George Grey in 1909. He was the 4th Earl Grey and served as governor general of Canada from 1904–11.

Earl Grey had planned to donate the cup as the reward for the amateur senior hockey competition in Canada, but Sir H. Montagu Allan stepped in and offered a trophy, the Allan Cup, for its prize. The first Grey Cup was won by the University of Toronto Varsity Blues.

Until 1921, the only competitors for the Grey Cup were teams from Ontario and Quebec. It was the early 1920s when teams from the west entered the competition. In 1936 the Western Interprovincial Football Union formed, consisting of teams from Alberta, Manitoba, and Saskatchewan.

Throughout the 1930s, and into the 1950s, amateur teams began to turn professional. The first team from the west to win the Grey Cup was the Winnipeg 'Pegs in 1935. They became the Winnipeg Blue Bombers the following season.

The league had paused from 1916–18 because of the conflict in the First World War. Following the Great War, a rules dispute with the Canadian Rugby Union meant there was no Grey Cup in 1919. The only other year without a CFL season or Grey Cup was 2020, during the global COVID-19 pandemic.

When Canada declared war on Germany in September 1939, an exodus of talent from the league became inevitable. The talent that enlisted were all-stars, players who were recognisable to fans and the Canadian public.

The league had just started to turn professional in the late 1930s. This meant that fans had begun to see some continuity at their clubs. It was not like the modern-day free agency where players move freely. The players of the 1930s were mainly local. They grew up in the area and represented their hometown teams. Some stars did travel but the bulk of rosters were made up of hometown talent. They were being paid and had no reason to leave.

Former CFL head statistician, Steve Daniel, said there were around 300 players that left the Canadian football competition to help the war effort. 'Canadian football in those days was much more of a community event,' said Daniel. 'If you look, even today, the Regina team, today's Saskatchewan Roughriders, Winnipeg Blue Bombers, Edmonton Elks, these teams are all still what we call community-owned. In those days, the Calgary [Bronks] team was also community-owned, as well as the BC Lions. That was all five western clubs.

'And with that community ownership, naturally, citizens had a stake in the team. It is a little like the kind of joke that is often told about the Saskatchewan Roughriders. They are a team with a very rabid following, and you will see a whole stadium of people wearing the same green jersey, wearing watermelons on their heads. There are people that will go to any lengths to show their allegiance to the team.

'Well, rewind to wartime, when food was short, and it was a group effort to survive, because so many Canadian resources were going to the war effort. Anything to pick up morale was really important. But even more so on the stage of community-owned teams.'

It seems unfathomable today what it must have been like living during a time when there was such a litany of bad news. For so many people, the league would have been a welcome distraction that provided a morale boost on the home front.

'Looking at newspaper reports from 1941–45,' Steve Daniel said, 'before you get to the sports section you are going past notices that you would rather not see, some of which will be closer to home.' The distraction of sport delivered a brief sense of normality with so much chaos and tragedy filling the radio broadcasts and printed press.

* * *

In January 1944, Canadian football's Eastern All-Star quarterback, Denis Whitaker, had his pick of major talent for the Tea Bowl game versus the USA.

'It really was an All-Star East-West team when we finally put it together,' he said. 'There was quite a few Toronto Argonauts stationed in Britain, including Captain George Hees, Captain Ken Turnbull, as well as Don Grant, a half-back, Bill Drinkwater, and Fred Brown. We were lucky to get Hulk Welsh, one of Canada's greatest punters, who played for the Hamilton Tigers and Montreal Wing Wheelers.'

The two-time Grey Cup winner and three-time Western All-Star, Jeff Nicklin, had also been brought in as the Canadians' back. Nicklin had played for the Winnipeg Blue Bombers from 1934–40, when he was enlisted. He was part of the Blue Bombers roster that had been the first West Division team to win the Grey Cup in 1935. That Winnipeg team made three more Grey Cup appearances, losing back-to-back in 1937 and 1938, before finally winning again in 1939.

Nicklin was at the height of his playing career in 1940 and could have continued in 1941, but instead he enlisted in the Army as a private. He was so impressive that he was recruited by the paratroopers. The four-time all-star and two-time Grey Cup winner finished playing football to jump out of aeroplanes into enemy territory and gunfire.

Fullback Andy Bieber was a team-mate of Nicklin's at the Blue Bombers and he won the Grey Cup with the club in the

1939 and 1941 seasons. Alongside these Winnipeg winners was another champion, Orville Burke, who won the Grey Cup with the Ottawa Rough Riders in 1940.

Added to the all-star cast of CFL icons who had found themselves far from home was Sarnia native, Nick Paithouski. Paithouski was a centre who played for Queen's University. Following graduation, he signed professionally with the Sarnia 2/26 Battery and later the Saskatchewan Roughriders. He was nominated the All-Star centre for Sarnia in 1940.

Paul 'Pappy' Rowe of the Calgary Bronks (later the Calgary Stampeders) was another All-Star back. Rowe played college football for Oregon, which meant he had experience of the American game, and would be inducted into the CFL Hall of Fame after his glittering career had ended.

There were around 30 players signed up for the Canadian Mustangs. Their coach was Major Chicks Mundell, a doctor in the Army Medical Corps. Mundell had played football at Queen's and coached Denis Whitaker at RMC. Their training was hard, but it was a welcome break from the rigours of the war.

'At that time in the war, not much was happening,' Denis Whitaker's daughter, Gail Whitaker Thompson, told me.

'They were waiting, waiting, waiting. So, this was actually a very good way for them to wait. Playing football and keeping their minds off the fact that they never knew when they would come back from the war.'

Before the war, these were the guys who helped to create the foundation of the Canadian game. They were the pioneers who revolutionised the sport into the competition we recognise today. Aspects of the game that we take for granted, for example, forward passing, had not become legal until 1931. Football had been like rugby prior to that period, in that players could only pass laterally. These players had been part of the evolution. They changed how to hold the football and derived how to block.

That band of brave men was part of the foundation of the CFL. The modern league boasts millions of fans, sold-out stadiums and international television deals that are worth amounts that would have been beyond their imaginations. If it was not for those revolutionaries who gave up their careers to fight for the Crown, we might not have the product as we know it today.

CHAPTER 4

Pearl Harbor

'At half-time, it started to leak in the locker rooms, but nobody was really sure of the magnitude'

– Joe Horrigan, former executive director of the Pro Football Hall of Fame

THERE WERE three football games being played that fateful day on December 7, 1941. News was not as instantaneous then as it is today, so while Pearl Harbor was being attacked, the fans in the stadiums were none the wiser.

'News was trickling out,' Joe Horrigan, the former executive director and historian at the Pro Football Hall of Fame told me when I met him at the museum in Canton, Ohio. Up until 2020, Joe had worked at the Hall of Fame for 42 years and was one of its longest-serving employees.

'Indications were happening during the game that those in the know suspected something serious had happened because they began to page over the public address system,' said Horrigan.

'They were calling for military personnel, high-ranking military personnel, government officials and such. Even some of the newspaper editors were paged at games to return to their offices.'

That was a clear indication to the reporters that there was serious breaking news taking place. Obviously, those people knew at the time what it would probably be about,' Joe Horrigan said, 'but the fans and the public, really, were not hearing this.'

The radio broadcasts for the games were interrupted with the breaking news, but the public were not taking radio sets into stadiums in 1941. The football games continued, the fans in the stands cheered, or moaned, and everything to them was normal. 'So, it was pretty much all systems go,' added Joe.

'At half-time, it started to leak in the locker rooms and there started to be some rumours that something was happening, but nobody was really sure of the magnitude, or of the validity of what was being said.'

One of the games being played that day was the Chicago Bears vs. Chicago Cardinals. In 2016, the *Chicago Tribune* produced a 'Chicago Flashback' feature on how fans heard of the news at that game. According to the article, Wallace Rosenbaum was nearly 15 years old and had been in the stadium with three friends. They had free tickets, courtesy of the *Chicago Times*.

Rosenbaum told the *Tribune* in 2016, 'We took three streetcars to get to Comiskey Park. We were sitting where they put the kids.'

It was Week 14 and the Bears made it a sweep of the Cardinals with a 34-24 road win. Coached by George Halas, the Chicago Bears went 5-0-0 on the road that season and finished with an overall regular season record of 10-1-0. Their city rivals fared much worse, however, with a 3-7-1 record. Coached by Jimmy Conzelman, the Cardinals were winless at home that campaign.

Rosenbaum said fans in the stadium were not informed about the Pearl Harbor attack. He and his friends learned that their country was at war when they were greeted by newsboys hawking extras outside the gates as they exited.

Another early kick-off that day was at New York's Polo Grounds, where the Brooklyn Dodgers were on the road to the New York Giants. The Dodgers existed as an NFL team from 1930 to 1943. In 1944 they were known as the Brooklyn Tigers, before merging with the Boston Yanks in 1945.

The Dodgers were a good team. They had a superstar quarterback in Ace Parker. Parker was a dual threat QB and had been gifted with a leg for punting. Before the Dodgers drafted Ace in the second round of the 1937 draft, they'd had two winning seasons out of eight. The three seasons prior to his selection were all losing campaigns. Ace was also a professional Major League Basball (MLB) player with the Philadelphia Athletics. He competed in both sports in 1937 and 1938.

The A's moved to Kansas City in 1955 and eventually settled in Oakland in 1968, which has been their home for more than 55 years. At the end of 2023 the League approved their move to Las Vegas in 2028.

Ace Parker won NFL MVP (Most Valuable Player) honours in 1940. The summer before that season he broke his ankle playing baseball. Parker played the first three games of that season with a 10-pound brace on his lower leg. Despite the handicap, he had his highest rushing season (306 yards) and led the Dodgers to their first winning season in seven years. They went 8-3-0, which was second in the Eastern Conference behind the 9-2-0 Washington Redskins. The Redskins advanced to the Championship Game as conference winners and were thrashed 73-0 by the Chicago Bears. That score still remains the biggest blowout in NFL history.

More than 55,000 people were in the Polo Grounds for the Dodgers vs. Giants game on December 7, 1941. Home fans were celebrating 'Tuffy Leemans Day', in honour of their star fullback who had been named first or second all-team since he was drafted second overall in 1936.

According to the *New York Daily News*, just as the ceremonial speeches honouring Leemans had finished and the game kicked off, Japanese planes were bombing Pearl Harbor. It was the Dodgers' back, Pug Manders, who stole the show on the field. Manders ended the season as the league's leading rusher. He scored a hat-trick of touchdowns in this game, including a pick six, to give Brooklyn a 21-0 lead. The final score was 21-7, but the Giants had already won the Eastern Division and the news coming from Hawaii put everything into perspective.

Confusion and anxiety swept the crowd when an urgent call for Colonel William J. Donovan to contact his office was relayed over the public address system. Calls for military and government officials then followed. Pages and tickers were sent to reporters in the press box, while supporters were left to question what the crisis was. Reports say that most of the people did not learn what had happened until they got home.

The Dodgers, with Ace Parker, had their first back-to-back winning seasons. Meanwhile, the Giants played the Chicago Bears in the Championship Game and lost 31-9. Parker's pro football career paused in 1942 when he went off to fight in the war with the Navy. He returned to the gridiron in 1946 and had a Hall of Fame career.

Parker was the first member of the Hall of Fame to live past their 100th birthday. He died in 2013, aged 101.

Alphonse 'Tuffy' Leemans retired from professional football in 1943. He was inducted into the Pro Football Hall of Fame in 1978. Less than six months after his induction he died of a heart attack. Leemans was 66.

* * *

The other game taking place on December 7, 1941, was the Washington Redskins at the Philadelphia Eagles. As at New York's Polo Grounds, this match-up kicked off at 2pm Easter Time around the time the Japanese began to bomb Pearl Harbor.

As far as the game was concerned, it was just a formality because the New York Giants had already clinched the Eastern Division. In an article for the Washington Commanders' website in 2015 headlined 'Flashback: A Forgotten Washington-Philly Game', Mike Richman, the author of *The Redskins Encyclopaedia* and the *Washington Redskins Football Vault*, wrote that the game at DC's Griffith Stadium had been clouded with confusion in the stands, much like at Chicago and New York.

Richman referenced the accounts from the late Shirley Povich, a former *Washington Post* columnist. There were over 27,000 fans gathered for the game as announcements began to call out, including requests such as, 'Admiral W.H.P. Bland is asked to report to his office at once!'

The appeals were sobering for the fans who had congregated in the stands to watch a football game. Calls for 'the resident commissioner of the Philippines, Mr Joaquim Eilzalde', who was 'urged to report to his office immediately!' provoked speculation between supporters.

'Joseph Umglumph of the Federal Bureau of Investigation is requested to report to the FBI office at once.'

'Capt. R.X. Fenn of the United States Army is asked to report to his office at once.'

The announcements over the public address system became increasingly frequent. Suddenly the Eagles and Redskins were the last thing on people's minds.

According to the Commanders article, the former Redskins lineman, and two-time Pro Bowler, Clyde Shugart said, 'We sensed that something happened, and everybody in the stands realized there was something wrong. But we didn't know what.'

Shirley Povich began covering sports for the *Washington Post* in 1922. In 1991 he wrote about his memories of that infamous day. 'For a few moments it was our exclusive secret,' Povich wrote. He recalled that another announcement rang out, 'Mr J. Edgar Hoover is asked to report to his office.'

Photographers were told to leave the game and head to the White House and Japanese embassy. Just one of them remained by the end of half-time. At the end of the game, fans were greeted by newsboys shouting 'Extra!' with the headlines 'US at War!' on the front pages.

For almost the entirety of the Eagles vs. Redskins contest, which lasted over three hours, fans at Griffith Park had been oblivious to the fact their country had been attacked. The Redskins owner, George Preston Marshall, ordered his staff not to make a public announcement to the crowd. When asked about his decision, Marshall said, 'I did not want to divert the fans' attention from the game.'

Mike Richman wrote in his 'Flashback' piece that the Redskins players were patriotic in their response. After the game, a group of them protested the attack by marching on the Japanese embassy in Washington. 'We wanted to square the account if they were looking for a fist fight,' former player Clyde Shugart said.

The Redskins beat the Eagles 20-14 and finished third in the Eastern Division with a record of 6-5-0. For the Eagles, it was a season to forget, as they went 2-8-1. Only the Pittsburgh Steelers had a worse record than them in the division. Those two Pennsylvania teams would merge a couple of seasons later in a collaboration to keep the league going during the war effort.

The following day, Monday, December 8, the United States of America officially entered World War II.

CHAPTER 5

NFL Carries On

'Football was used as a rallying point and place where people could go cheer, they would instil a sense of patriotism and teamwork'

– Joe Horrigan, former executive director of the Pro Football Hall of Fame

MORE THAN 600 NFL players served in the US armed forces during the Second World War.

There was consideration early on that pro football in America should suspend operations out of respect for what was happening around the world. However, officials agreed that the best thing to do was to keep the league going so that they could depict normalcy as much as possible for the American public. They could also use football as a rallying point and place where people could go cheer. Football, in their view, would instil a sense of patriotism and teamwork throughout the war effort.

On the field they had enlistments from players after games, along with fundraisers to raise money for war bonds, the war effort and relief funds. While football was acknowledging the war effort, it was also trying to maintain normality in the country at a level that was acceptable and respectful.

But there was also a player shortage due to the volume of talent that had enlisted or been drafted to serve. In response, the league established the 'NFL War Relief Fund' in 1942. This collection aimed to raise money for the war effort, providing financial support for various initiatives.

Generally, across America the feeling was very positive as they entered the Second World War. The troops were sent off as heroes with people lining the streets to cheer them as they marched on parade. Following the atrocities at Pearl Harbor, there was a belief that fighting was something that they had to do because their country had been attacked so ferociously.

Young men were supported by the people at home, and mothers would proudly wear pins to show how many members of their family were bravely serving.

Despite the early optimism, and notably as the war continued, the American public found itself in need of respite, and much of that came through sport. In 1942, the United States was facing unprecedented challenges on the global stage, and the home front was equally affected by the war effort. During this turbulent period, the NFL played a remarkable role in boosting American morale.

That 1942 season was a far cry from the multi-billion-dollar industry we know today. It was a relatively young league, having been founded in 1920, and was still struggling to establish itself as a major sport in the American consciousness. The war had already taken its toll on the league, with so many players and fans enlisting to fight. Despite these challenges, the league pressed on, determined to provide entertainment and a sense of unity for a nation in turmoil.

It was the first season since American forces embarked for combat around the world, so the introduction of the 'taxi squad' had been introduced. The taxi squad was a group of players who were not on active rosters but were available to be called up in case of injuries or player shortages due to military service. This allowed teams to maintain a semblance of competitive balance while their rosters were constantly changing.

There were only ten NFL teams in the 1940s, compared to the 32 that compete today. Teams were desperately trying to fill their rosters. George Halas, who was the head coach and owner of the Chicago Bears, recalled that his team would hold try-outs and sign 'anyone who could run around the field twice'. His team were reigning champions heading into 1942.

Halas himself left the Bears in mid-season to join the Navy. Luke Johnsos and Heartly (Hunk) Anderson served as co-coaches, steering the team to an 11-0 regular season record.

One of the remarkable aspects of that NFL season was the high level of play that was maintained despite the challenges faced by teams. The Washington Redskins, led by quarterback Sammy Baugh, were particularly dominant during that campaign. Baugh, one of the greatest quarterbacks in NFL history, had an outstanding ability to throw the ball with precision and power that was unparalleled at the time, and he played a crucial role in preserving the Redskins' success.

Not only could he throw the ball, but he was also an efficient kicker. From 1940 to 1943, Baugh led the league in punting for four straight seasons.

The Green Bay Packers' Cecil Isbell led the league in passing during that first wartime NFL season, with 2,021 yards and 24 touchdowns. Baugh was second with 1,524 passing yards and 11 touchdowns, followed by the Philadelphia Eagles' Tommy Thompson, who threw for 1,410 yards and eight touchdowns. All three were selected for the Pro Bowl, but only Baugh was made All-Pro out of that trio. Sammy Baugh had the best passing accuracy in the league, completing 132 of 225 attempts (58.7 per cent accuracy).

Baugh's performance was not only remarkable on the field, but he was also inspirational for fans watching across the country. He became a symbol of excellence and determination right through a period when those qualities were desperately needed. The Redskins finished the season 10-1.

The league's superstar of that era was Green Bay Packers legend, Don Hutson. Hutson played his entire 11-year career with the Packers. A versatile player, he could operate on both sides of the ball, as a safety and receiver. In 1942 he led the league in receiving yards (1,211) and touchdowns (17). His former team-mate, Bernie Scherer, later labelled him 'the Jerry Rice of his era'.

Many believe that the modern-day wide receiver evolved from Hutson. In 1945 he scored 29 points in a single quarter against the Detroit Lions. That record still stands as the most points scored by an NFL player in one quarter. The future Hall of Famer won consecutive league MVP honours in 1941 and 1942. He scored 99 touchdowns in his career, leading the league in receptions in eight of his 11 seasons. If that wasn't enough, he also made 30 interceptions.

Green Bay finished second in the Western Conference behind the Chicago Bears in 1942. The season culminated with the Bears facing the Redskins in the Championship Game. It was played at Washington's Griffith Stadium on December 13. The Bears were on the hunt for their third consecutive title, while the Redskins were out to avenge the 73-0 drubbing by Chicago in the Championship Game two years earlier. Sammy Baugh threw the only touchdown pass, and the Redskins won 14-6.

The role of newspapers and radio commentaries in promoting NFL games cannot be overstated. In the absence of television broadcasts, radio play-by-play announcers like Bob Elson and Bill Stern painted vivid pictures of the games for those unable to attend. Those broadcasts brought the excitement and drama of football into living rooms across the nation, fostering a sense of unity and shared experience.

The Championship Game drew a record crowd of 36,006 spectators, reflecting the importance of football in American life during the war. Despite the pressure and the high stakes, the players delivered an exciting and hard-fought contest. The 1942 NFL season was more than just a collection of football games; it was a symbol of hope and resilience. It demonstrated that even in the darkest of times, sports could serve as a beacon of light, bringing people together.

Teams faced enormous pressure to continue in 1943, but the league found a way to keep going.

CHAPTER 6

The Steagles

'All it meant was we had twice as many lousy players'

– Philadelphia Eagles Hall of Fame tackle, Al Wistert

IN 1943, the war was taking its toll on everyone around the world. Huge sacrifices were being made to support the armed forces and to remain functional throughout all aspects of domestic life, including professional sports. In America, the NFL was not exempt from this and the league faced several challenges as it attempted to maintain its operations during that period.

The Cleveland Rams' co-owners, Dan Reeves and Frederick Levy Junior, were serving in the military; therefore, the league granted the franchise permission to suspend operations for the season.

This was the year that the NFL made wearing helmets mandatory. The league had also agreed to a ten-game season. Free substitution was adopted as part of new rules and regulations.

Two teams that were struggling to field full rosters were the Philadelphia Eagles and Pittsburgh Steelers. To help keep the NFL functional, these Pennsylvania franchises chose to merge. The league granted permission for the move to go ahead on June 19 of that year. For one year only they were known as Phil-Pitt, although they will forever be known as the Steagles, the name given to them by fans.

Speaking in an interview in 1974, the late Steelers owner, Art Rooney Senior, explained the reason for the merger: 'It was done out of necessity. The war was going on and most of the players were in the service. A lot of the coaches, too. We did not have the manpower to field a team and neither did the Eagles, but we thought we could make it work if we pooled our resources.'

Besides having a manpower shortage, those two teams had a terrible record on the gridiron to begin with. From a business standpoint, it made sense because it helped keep both franchises afloat. But from the fan perspective, it made cheering for the team that much more difficult. The Steagles had to divide home games between the two cities. On today's roads with faster cars, the journey is 304 miles and takes around five hours. In 1943 that was taking much longer.

As part of the war effort, it was mandatory for players to work at least 40 hours a week, which impacted practice, as well as the squad being split on either side of the state. Those players were not granted the luxuries of the modern-day athletes, who have their sports scientists, scheduled rest time, and nutritionists. Many had to do arduous hours of manual labour before heading to practice to learn play designs alongside team-mates they barely knew.

According to the players, the biggest issue the team had was with the coaches. It had been decided that Eagles head coach Greasy Neale, and Steelers head coach Walt Kiesling, would co-coach the team. The late Vic Sears, an All-Pro offensive lineman with the Eagles, said in an interview that featured on the Philadelphia Eagles' website, 'Greasy would tell him off and Kiesling would come back at him, and we'd be there wondering when we would get back to work. It was the craziest thing I ever saw in all my years of football, but we finished with a winning record. Do not ask me how.'

When I spoke to Joe Horrigan at the Pro Football Hall of Fame, he told me, 'One player once put it that "we took two bad teams, merged them together and made them worse".'

That player was the Hall of Fame tackle, Al Wistert. Wistert was a rookie that season. Speaking years later, he said, 'All it meant was we had twice as many lousy players. Look at the teams. The Eagles had never had a winning season and the Steelers were almost as bad.'

The Eagles' Pro Bowl quarterback from the previous season, Tommy Thompson, was drafted into the Army in 1942 and served in Europe until the end of the war.

The award-winning writer and NFL producer, Ray Didinger, author of *The Eagles Encyclopaedia: Champions Edition*, wrote that the Steagles acquired quarterback Ray Zimmerman from the Washington Redskins as a replacement. Zimmerman was backup to Sammy Baugh and the League convinced the Redskins to sell him to the Pennsylvania team.

Zimmerman threw for 846 yards, nine touchdowns and 17 interceptions in that 1943 season. Only two quarterbacks threw more touchdown passes than Zimmerman that year. They were the Bears' Sid Luckman (28 TD) and Baugh (23 TD). The Steagles' passer started nine of ten games for them, completing 43 of 124 pass attempts, which was a completion rate of 34 per cent. He had a quarterback rating of 44.

The Steagles' solo NFL campaign turned out better than most would have hoped, given the circumstances. It was an inconsistent year: they started off 2-0 with a 17-0 win over the Brooklyn Dodgers that was followed by a 28-14 victory over the New York Giants the next week. If they thought it was going to be easy, they were brought back down to earth with a bang in Week 3, losing 48-21 to the Chicago Bears.

The Giants had their revenge over the Steagles in Week 4 with a resounding 42-14 triumph.

The Steagles were not a great team in terms of on-field performances, but they weren't terrible. In fact, achieving a winning season [5-4-1] was something the Philadelphia Eagles had never managed to do.

Regardless of the team's struggles on and off the field, the Steagles were symbolic of how far the teams and society were willing to go in a bid to keep things as normal as possible across the country.

CHAPTER 7

American Football on Foreign Fields

'Come in your thousands and see two crack American sides in the first big game of American Football ever played in this country'

– Press promotion, Northern Ireland, 1942

AMERICAN FOOTBALL was played between US military personnel throughout the Second World War. The first game took place as early as November 14, 1942.

It was contested at Ravenhill Stadium in Belfast, Northern Ireland. Newspaper advertisements encouraged locals to head out in their thousands and watch the spectacle. The rugby-mad locals will have left the stadium that Saturday evening feeling befuddled by what they experienced on the field.

More than 8,000 people packed into the venue for the game, which made a good return on ticket sales. Revenue from the tickets went to the benefit of Royal Victoria Hospital in Belfast and the Soldiers', Sailors', Airmen's Families' Association.

No sooner had the American armed forces arrived in Northern Ireland than they were making a positive impact on the local area. Organisers presented more than £730 to the hospital and Association, which was a phenomenal amount considering there was rationing throughout that period.

The match-up pitted the Yarvards against the Hales. The eagle-eyed will spot the play on words by the jovial organisers (in reference to the Ivy League universities of Harvard and Yale). The Yarvards were captained by their fullback, Corporal Robert Hopfer. The game report from the *Stars and Stripes* newspaper on November 16 said that Hopfer was instrumental for them in the second quarter of the contest.

Hopfer's team was 6-0 down in Belfast, and he took the ball on every play in that second quarter, registering three first downs and a touchdown. The Yarvards took the lead with the resulting extra point. They went in at half-time 7-6 up. The star fullback, however, was forced to exit the game after the interval with an injury. A field goal for Hale in that same period was enough to win the contest 9-7. The Yarvards had their chances, but the receivers struggled with their catching.

The American cheerleaders in the crowd may have engaged the local support more than the action on the field. It was reported that the Belfast residents did not even know the score when they left the stadium.

Information had been generously provided for the curious observers. Gameday programmes included the rules to help the locals understand what was going on. The Americans certainly did their homework on the rugby-loving nation, opening the introduction with a comparison between American football and its cousin.

The introduction read, 'As you view American Football for the first time, I am certain you will be impressed by its similarity to your great game of "Rugger."' They may not have won the crowd over with the product on the field, but the Americans certainly charmed their hosts long before kick-off. The rest of the programme included three pages of rules, from point-scoring to scrimmages and turnovers. There was even an image of the gridiron to improve the Irish knowledge.

The report from a journalist at *Ireland's Saturday Night*, a Northern Ireland sports newspaper, did little to sell the sport to prospective fans. He wrote, 'The game started off very slowly, and there was some rather sloppy ball playing until near the end of the first quarter when Cpl. Robert Hopfer, captain of the Yarvard team, missed a punt, and Frank Back, half-back of the Hale side, recovered the punt. He then attempted a field goal, which missed.'

Americans were attempting to showcase the best of their sport for the people who had been so generous in giving up their homes and land to help them in the war effort. The game may have been baffling, but it provided respite for a few thousand locals and contributed massively with its charity fundraising. This was the first of many games staged in the UK and beyond throughout the conflict.

With so many college and professional football players serving abroad, almost every military base from Army to Navy, Air Corps to Marine had their pick of high-calibre players when games were played.

* * *

A notable game that introduced Londoners to the gridiron took place at White City Stadium near Shepherd's Bush on May 8, 1943. The game was again used as a fundraiser for charity, as most events had been during the war. Money from ticket and programme sales for this contest went to the British Red Cross for Prisoners of War Fund. The *Stars and Stripes* newspaper on the day prior to the game had a section that provided the best directions to the stadium, including bus services to and from the ground from central

London. There was certainly a sense of anticipation for the spectacle.

America's finest were on show for the 25,000 spectators that Saturday afternoon in west London. Events began half an hour before the 'Crimson Tide' and the 'Fighting Irish' kicked off. Although the teams bore the names of famed college teams, Alabama and Notre Dame respectively, the Crimson Tide were made up of members of the Field Artillery from Pennsylvania and its surrounding states. Their 'fierce' opposition, the Fighting Irish, had men from the Engineers who were recruited from the Midwestern states.

There was music from the London Base Command band and the Artillery unit's musicians, who played fanfare and colour while British Red Cross nurses, Auxiliary Territorial Service (ATS) women, the Women's Royal Naval Service and other female organisations paraded the field.

The players had an intense two-hour practice session at the venue the day before, which showed how seriously the game was being taken by everyone involved. Both sides had met the previous year in Belfast, when the Fighting Irish won 14-0, much to the delight of the local crowd.

English spectators, like the locals who attended the Yarvards vs. Hale game in Belfast, were left feeling confused by what they witnessed. Though Londoners agreed it was a tough sport, they found it dull and tame. And, as you get with American football today, there were complaints about the stop-start nature of the game.

The contest itself was won by the Crimson Tide, who avenged their humbling loss in Northern Ireland with a 19-6 victory. A member of the Crimson Tide was Private First-Class John W. Kelly from Harrisburg, Pennsylvania. He wrote a letter about the match-up to his local paper, the *Harrisburg Telegraph*. Included with the letter was a gameday programme. Kelly reported that the British press showed little interest in the game. The article read, 'English sports fans jammed into White City Stadium, London, to watch the game. Accounts of the game that featured in the Isle's newspapers and magazines gave more attention to the individual action of the fans and the players than in the description of the game or the score, which in many cases was relegated to the last few paragraphs of the stories.'

The back page of the programme displayed the rules for the American football newbies in the crowd. Little did they know that 80 years later, crowds would be queuing in their thousands at Wembley Stadium, just a few miles away, to cheer their favourite NFL stars, donning the jerseys of their teams, and cheering every yard, tackle, catch and run. It would have been beyond the Americans' wildest dreams that the MVP of their league would be playing in Germany, where people queued in their millions to be able to purchase a ticket.

Victory meant so much to the Crimson Tide, *Stars and Stripes* reported, that Corporal Robert Hopfer – yes, he was at it again – and his team-mates were heard celebrating in the locker room. Hopfer had opened the scoring for his team in the fourth quarter, all their points being scored in the final period. The team was presented with a two-handled silver cup as their prize. Players tried to borrow money from anybody they thought was rich enough, in the hope that they could celebrate their triumph.

* * *

The European Theater of Operations was born in 1943. Corporal Robert D. Hopfer's Crimson Tide were the champions, which is why their celebrations were likened to those of the Brooklyn Dodgers' World Series victories. The Tide had beaten every team they played that year, including that momentous day at White City. They only played three games, but the trophy and jubilations felt a million miles from the horrors of the front line.

There were multiple championships and trophies at stake for different divisions. From 1943 through to the end of the Second World War, games were played in Leeds, Nottingham, Bristol, Paris, even Marseille and Oran in Algeria. In Paris, 20,000 spectators filed into Parc des Princes on December 19, 1944, for a pre-Christmas classic between the Ninth Air Force and First General Hospital. The French capital had been liberated months earlier, on August 25. Any hopes of attracting French fans to the sport were soon dashed by a low-scoring contest that ended 6-0.

Details of the Arba Bowl in Algeria have been documented in Wilbur D. Jones's book, *Football! Navy! War! How Military 'Lend-Lease' Players Saved the College Game and Helped Win World War II.*

Jones quoted this description of the game between the Oran Refrigeration Termites and Casablanca Ordnance Rabchasers: 'Here in San Phillipe beside the sparkling waters of the Mediterranean, some 15,000 grid-hungry generals, admirals, nurses, WACs (Women's Army Corps), soldiers and sailors – and a fair-sized sprinkling of high French and Arab dignitaries – witnessed the first double-header football bowl game ever played.'

The actress Rosalind Russell, and four army enlisted women were queens. Jones Junior also wrote that there was camel and burro racing with WACs as jockeys, WAC drills and reviews, martial music, and a camera field day.

Football's nuances with the military served as a release for the young men abroad, and at home, but especially on foreign fields where there was a lot of waiting and not a lot of action. They had the relentless training, but that had become monotonous for so many. These were young twenty-somethings who wanted a taste of action. So, the chance to team up with comrades and line up against other regiments served as a welcome distraction and physical release.

'It was also the case in boxing matches and wrestling matches,' said Richard Crepeau, Professor Emeritus of History at the University of Central Florida, Orlando, 'which were also very common in the military. Although the NFL is the number one sport in America now, and hugely popular around the world, American football was not the attraction it is today.'

Therefore, in terms of competition, and in the camps and bases overseas during the 1940s, baseball was much more commonly used as a form of recreation for the servicemen, whereas football was a training technique.

Baseball was the entertainment, and remained America's number one sport until 1960, and so it did everything possible to promote patriotism. Major League Baseball shipped equipment, and the *Sporting News* shipped their weekly issue overseas to every serviceman possible. So, baseball infiltrated itself into that culture very heavily.

The NFL didn't have anything comparable, but they sent some equipment. If they had not, then *The Greatest American Football Story that has Never Been Told* would not exist.

'The National Football League did raise money for bond drives,' Crepeau said, 'but never on the scale that baseball was able to do.

'Whereas today the NFL would be all over it, raising money in the millions and flags covering the fields before kick-off.'

There were commanders at various bases who saw sport as an extremely important part of their programme. Both football and baseball were competitions that were top of their team activities, with baseball number one. Both sports offered important bonding exercises and gave a focus to men away from the battlefield and their rigorous military training.

These commanders would browse the enlistment lists and cherry-pick the athletes they felt would deliver key victories on the field of play. Some players were left waiting to be sent overseas because their skills as athletes were deemed so important to certain bases and military teams at home.

After the end of the war a baseball game was played in Hawaii. It was a faux All-Star match-up between the service stars of the American League and National League, played at Honolulu's Furlong Field, near Pearl Harbor.

A few of the players hadn't been demobilised from their respective operations in the Pacific, so suddenly these teams in Hawaii were welcoming people from all over the United States and Europe, some of whom were being shipped to them a day or two before the big game.

A local paper wrote that the Navy series would 'present more individual stars than even the World Series on the mainland … a titanic battle between some of the best-known players in baseball'.

Similar examples occurred in football, with players essentially being captured by military commanders and, one may argue, held as a hostage to winning. Long before the multi-billion-dollar corporation of sport, there was a business of sport among military commanders who were desperate to win at whatever cost was necessary. Which made it not uncommon to see a man with a suntan lining up on an English sports field in the middle of winter.

SECTION 2:

The Stars of the Show

CHAPTER 8

All-Star Line-Up

'London's huge White City Stadium never saw such a game'

– Newspaper report on the Tea Bowl, 1944

THERE WAS a plethora of talent on the Canadian and American teams that played in the Tea Bowl on February 13, 1944. Over the next few pages, we will learn more about the standout performers from that game, and the Coffee Bowl rematch that took place on March 19. Both match-ups were played at London's White City Stadium in front of crowds that exceeded the numbers seen at NFL Championship Games and CFL Grey Cups.

As each man who featured in those London contests would stress, all the players were stars and heroes in both football and battle.

What I have learned from researching this story is that every serviceman risked all that they had for this war. Each one of them had put their life on the line to fight in a conflict they did not want. They were all humble about their bravery.

Every individual would quickly highlight the heroics of others before they could take any credit for their own courage. That could also be true on the football field. Whether it was on the gridiron or the battlefield, each man had a job to do, it was regimented, they worked as a unit and achieved their goal as one.

Throughout this section we get to learn about the key players of these games. We discover the sacrifices they made to their football careers and family. There is celebration and tragedy. But the games were never about those individuals. No man's story is greater than the other. Therefore, I chose to include this chapter to honour the men who also made an impact on the field at White City Stadium in February and March 1944. The latter game took place just seven weeks before D-Day and the Allied invasion of France.

Lieutenant Orville Burke (Canada), quarterback, Ottawa Rough Riders

Out of the 110 editions of the Canadian Football League showpiece, there are just ten quarterbacks that have started in four Grey Cup games and Orville Burke is one of them.

He was Irish and had grown up in Ottawa. Most of his early life was spent in the Canadian capital. Burke attended St Patrick's College in Ottawa from 1933 to 1935. He played quarterback for their football team and led them through an undefeated season in '35.

The Ottawa Rough Riders signed him in 1936. Burke did not see much action on the field that season, as the Rough Riders marched to the Grey Cup. They lost the final 26-20 to the Sarnia Imperials.

He was handed the reins at quarterback the following year and led the team with distinction for the next four seasons. For a period, Orville Burke was forced to live with the infamy of a blunder he had made during the 1939 Grey Cup against the Winnipeg Blue Bombers.

The 22-year-old's football world came crashing down in the biggest moment of all, when he fumbled the ball deep into Winnipeg territory. Snow had been falling all game, the ground was frozen, and points were at a premium. The score was tied at 7-7 with the game heading to overtime, but Burke's mishap proved to be a valuable turnover for Winnipeg, who scored on the resulting drive and won the contest with seconds remaining.

He got his redemption the following season, as the Rough Riders beat the Toronto Balmy Beach by an aggregate score of 20-7 over a two-game showpiece.

In 1941 Burke led Ottawa to their third consecutive Grey Cup appearance. On November 29 he took to the field against the Blue Bombers and was hungry for revenge. The game was almost two years to the day from the mistake that had continued to haunt him.

As expected, much of the build-up to the 1941 final was dominated by Burke's revenge and that fateful play. 'That score two years ago was too close to be decisive,' Burke said in the days leading up to the Grey Cup. He added, 'Every Ottawa player who took part in that game has been gunning for another shot at the Bombers ever since.'

'No doubt about it,' Burke said, 'that fumble in 1939 was the most disastrous one I ever made. It was just an ordinary fumble, that's all, and there weren't any alibis.'

Burke suffered a bad injury to his lip during the game, severely cutting it when hit by a Winnipeg player in the second quarter. Luck was not on the Rough Riders' side against their nemesis from the west. Ottawa had an opportunity to exact revenge in the closing stages with a 15-yard field goal. However, their kicker, George Fraser, missed it. 'I guess I lost my bearings,' said Fraser after the game.

The kick would have pulled Ottawa level with Winnipeg at 18-18, but football is a game of yards played by inches. And the ball sailed just inches past the post. Disaster again for Burke and his team-mates.

'I can't tell you exactly what happened,' said the kicker. 'But I'll tell you this, the snap was good, and the ball was well held for me.' Fraser also added, 'It was just like golf. I lifted my head; I did everything wrong.'

Throughout that Grey Cup run, Burke was also coaching his old college team. He took up the role at the start of the football season. Jack Koffman from the *Ottawa Citizen* wrote on September 4, 1941, 'St Patrick's College choice of Orville Burke as coach of their football teams this fall is to be commended. Orv played a lot of good games for the green shirts in other years, and his knowledge of the sport, as well as his interest in the game, stamps him as a suitable person to be helping schoolboy aspirants.'

Following the Grey Cup defeat in 1941, Burke joined the Canadian Army. He was an Armoured Corps man, became a lieutenant and was posted to the 21st Canadian Armoured Regiment. As he fought through the Second World War, he was promoted to captain.

On April 10, 1945, Burke and his tank company were in the small German town of Sogel. Sogel is a municipality to the north-west of the country, about 30 miles from the Dutch border.

Burke's company were eating breakfast when they were alerted to the sound of machine-gun fire. Fifteen hours earlier, Canadian armoured troops had passed through the town as they made their advance to north-east Germany across the plain near the Netherlands. Some had taken up residence in the hotel for the night and had been afforded the rare luxury of an uninterrupted night's sleep.

While a few troops were munching on their bacon and eggs that Tuesday morning, comrades rushed into the hotel with rifles on their shoulders, heeding the warning that German paratroopers were attacking.

The hotel became the defence point. Word spread that there were only six or seven Germans in the town, but soon that number had become 30, and others reported that three enemy paratrooper companies were advancing on the area.

Later confirmation reported that a German paratrooper battalion had pulled out from the Netherlands and concentrated on a town north of Sogel. With the morning mist as their cover, teenage Germans headed towards the town, thinking it was lightly defended. The Canadian motor troops beat off two counter-attacks, with a few evasive Germans infiltrating the town. They were quickly surrounded.

Later that day, Burke's armoured regiment took out multiple units and vehicles, as well as German SS men, six miles east of Sogel. Burke had recently been made captain at this point. He was instrumental in stopping the Germans from rushing to the Ems River, a key crossing that they were trying to hold from the Allies.

Captain Burke was honoured for his services and made a Member of the Order of the British Empire (MBE).

Burke kept up his football whilst serving in Europe. As well as participating in the Tea Bowl game, he coached and played for the Fourth Division Atoms. The former Rough Riders quarterback assisted in handling the Canadian Army team in England, helping the unit win the Canadian Armed Forces title.

After the war, Burke returned to Canada and made a brief appearance for the Rough Riders. On the eve of the 1946 CFL season, Burke shattered the hearts of Rough Riders fans when he announced he was leaving. The Grey Cup-winning quarterback and war hero had accepted a job in Vancouver with a lumber firm. The job and its guaranteed salary were too good to turn down.

It was fitting that his final game was against the Hamilton Tigers in the season opener. The Tigers featured a couple of familiar faces from the Canadian Tea Bowl team, including Denis Whitaker and Nick Paithouski.

Ottawa lost a great quarterback. In discussing the move before his final game, Burke said it was a gut-wrenching decision to leave the city where he had spent most of his life.

He took up a coaching position in British Columbia, supervising junior football. He later took up a coaching job at the University of British Columbia Thunderbirds, before acquiring a role as mentor at Vancouver College.

Andy Bieber (Canada), running back, Winnipeg Blue Bombers

Andy Bieber was Winnipeg born and bred. Growing up, Bieber played high school football and was later coached by the Canadian Football Hall of Famer, Andrew Currie, during his college career. In 1965 Currie chaired the sub-committee which was responsible for the revision and re-writing of the Canadian Football League's Rule Book. This Rule Book was adopted in 1967.

Bieber graduated from college in 1938 and joined the Winnipeg Blue Bombers as a running back. The club had lost the Grey Cup to the Toronto Argonauts the previous season and returned to the final at the end of Bieber's first year. However, they were defeated again by Toronto, 30-7.

Bieber was given the fullback position in 1939 and Winnipeg went 10-2. He scored the only touchdown of the game at the Grey Cup, leading the Bombers to the trophy in an 8-7 victory. Reporters remarked on Bieber's 'tremendous' running, describing his slashing style as one of the highlights of the game.

There was no keeping Andy Bieber out of the end zone during the 1940 season. The star back was joint-leading points scorer, but the Bombers did not compete at the Grey Cup because of a dispute over differing rules between the East and West.

The 1941 season was shortened because of the war; Winnipeg finished the regular season 6-2. With their dispute resolved, they returned to the showpiece. Bieber claimed his second Grey Cup title.

Like so many Canadian football stars, he enlisted to serve in the war. Andy Bieber joined the Winnipeg Rifles. Just as his football acumen had elevated Bieber's success on the gridiron, the fullback's intelligence and leadership qualities helped him rise through the ranks of the army.

Bieber was involved in the Normandy landings on D-Day. The football star had been made lieutenant of his regiment and led them up Juno Beach.

Before he was discharged in 1945, Bieber had been promoted to major and later to lieutenant-colonel. After the war was won, he returned to education and studied at the University of Manitoba. He graduated as a chartered accountant and took up a position as controller of a lumber firm. It was different to the life he knew on the gridiron before the war, but he remained with the company until he retired in 1982.

Bieber spent a couple of years as a Canadian Football League official and landed the role as club director of the Blue Bombers in 1958. This Winnipeg native was proud of his team and derived great satisfaction from holding the position of team vice-president in the 1970s.

Just two months before Andy Bieber died, he was honoured by the club and installed into the Winnipeg Blue Bombers' Hall of Fame. The two-time Grey Cup winner died on November 18, 1985. He was 68.

Ken Turnbull (Canada), end, Toronto Argonauts.

Ken Turnbull was an Ontario native. He was born in Toronto in 1920 and grew up as a gifted sportsperson. During his years at Upper Canada College, he competed and excelled at boxing, cricket, hockey, rugby and football.

Therefore it was no surprise when he became a football player with Toronto Balmy Beach Football Club in 1941 at the age of 21. The Balmy Beach struggled that season, finishing third in the Eastern Canadian Union with a 2-4 record. Turnbull's CFL career was then put on hold as he enlisted to fight in the war.

Turnbull served with the Toronto Scottish Regiment and rose to the rank of captain. Turnbull was only 22 years of age when he went to war. The qualities he learned on the gridiron paved the way for success on the battlefront. The nuances common to football and the armed forces had paid dividends for another player, proving how great accomplishments can be achieved when working as a unit.

Following the war, Turnbull eventually returned to football and played for a season with the Toronto Argonauts. It became a fortuitous move for the star end, as he helped the Boatmen advance to the playoffs and win the Grey Cup. With a national title to his name, Turnbull began work in the packaging industry and started his own business. Turnbull Packaging was regarded as an innovative and cutting-edge company that had revolutionised the trade.

He was the eldest of four brothers and was married to Sarah for 57 years. His obituary read, 'Ken will always be remembered by all those whose lives he touched, for his engaging sense of humour, cutting wit and love of great conversation.'

Ken Turnbull died on September 14, 2008. The Toronto Argonauts paid tribute to their former champion in honour of the success he had with the club. He was 88.

Sir Edwin Leather (Canada), manager.

Edwin 'Ted' Leather managed the team of Canadians for the Tea Bowl in 1944. The Canuck left for England during the war in 1942 and liked it so much he decided to stay.

His name is well known in the UK for his role with the Conservative Party. He was elected as an MP in 1950 and served for 14 years until he was forced to retire because of ill health. Leather was picked to chair the first party conference after Edward Heath became prime minister in 1970.

The Canadian was not shy of speaking his mind and had been critical of the Americans during the Suez Crisis in 1956. Leather had accused them of undermining Britain when the Eisenhower administration pressured them and France into accepting a United Nations ceasefire with Egypt. The United States' public condemnation of their invasion of Egypt had soured relations with its former allies.

Ted Leather was born in Hamilton, Ontario. As a youngster he competed in gymnastics. He attended the Royal Military College Canada, where he spent his higher education studies. Leather was then commissioned into the Canadian Army in 1939 and had been one of the original officers of the 1st Canadian Parachute Battalion. Disaster struck, however, when he became seriously injured after his parachute failed in a training exercise. The young paratrooper spent nine months in a plaster cast.

As a result of his injuries, he served with the Toronto Scottish and Royal Artillery. In the years that followed, he devoted his time to organising gymnastics, training, and managed several Canadian Army athletics teams. He had also managed baseball and football for the troops in southern England, keeping them occupied as the monotony of training exercises for the impending invasion of Europe weighed on their young minds.

Leather also became a dab hand at broadcasting and would present a weekly programme for the Canadian Broadcasting Corporation. Generations later, Ted Leather could be heard making shrewd and witty contributions on the BBC radio programme *Any Questions?*

He was knighted in 1962, becoming a British citizen so as to be able to receive the honour. Leather was later appointed governor of Bermuda following the murder of Sir Richard Sharples. He retired from office in 1977, but rather than returning to England or Canada, stayed on the island to live a life of leisure. The former diplomat wrote several spy novels, including *The Vienna Elephant* (1977) and *The Duveen Letter* (1980).

Sir Edwin Leather died in Paget, Bermuda on April 5, 2005. He was 85.

CHAPTER 9

Jeff Nicklin

'If you could say words that would reflect Jeff Nicklin, it would be: Follow me'

– Steve Daniel, former CFL Head Statistician

JEFF NICKLIN was a natural winner. Born in Fort William, Ontario, he grew up in Winnipeg, Manitoba. It was in Winnipeg that he discovered football, and he was very good at it.

'What I would say about Jeff Nicklin is that he was one of the primary players in Canadian football in the 1930s,' Steve Daniel, the former CFL head statistician explained.

Nicklin was an All-Star of his time. By the age of 19 he broke into the Winnipeg team. The club was known as the Winnipegs until they became the Blue Bombers in 1935. Even at an early age, he was a young man dedicated to his craft. His sheer determination and drive would deliver him CFL honours. Later in life, he would swiftly rise up the ranks of the military throughout his service in the Second World War.

He could do anything on the football field. Nicklin had an athletic build that enabled him to dominate defences with the ball in his hands. His traits immediately draw comparisons to Christian McCaffrey, the San Francisco 49ers and former Stanford and Carolina Panthers running back. Nicklin's mesmerising runs on highlights videos display excellent vision, composure, and a natural ability to run through gaps. He had a solid physical frame that was accompanied with a square jaw, and a talent to operate as a receiver. He was a dual threat back who appeared to be ahead of his time on the football field.

His coach at the Blue Bombers, Reginald 'Red' Threlfall, moved Nicklin from an end position to the backfield in 1938. It was a move that saw the young star thrive.

Threlfall is regarded as one of the best coaches Winnipeg has had. His winning percentage of .778 remains the highest in the club's history. When commenting on Jeff Nicklin, Threlfall said, 'Jeff was as good as they come, and one of the better-developed Canadian football players.

'He was an exceptionally good blocker,and simply dynamite when going after passes.

'Jeff developed faster than most of the local boys. He had mature judgement and when things weren't going just quite right during a game, I could always find out from him what was wrong. Nicklin was always quick to take advantage of any opportunities on the football field and he never quit. It didn't matter to him if we were down 15 points with five minutes to play. He still thought we could win and played that way.'

Nicklin went straight from junior football and immediately headed into the Winnipeg team. He was part of the inaugural season of the Western Interprovincial Football Union in 1936. Here is a reminder that until that point, the Canadian Football League was made up of teams in the east of the country – anywhere east of Lake Superior and Lake Huron. The following year he was an All-Star.

Raised in the city, he was a local lad whom everyone revered, from the stands and in the locker room. Joe Ryan, Nicklin's general manager at the Blue Bombers, wrote in a local newspaper, 'Probably it is because, after our associations with Jeff, we rated him almost immortal. We were sure no German Hitlerite could ever get him down – any more than we were always sure that the hardest tackler could ever drop Jeff low.'

Two years after Jeff's, and Winnipeg's, first Grey Cup win, they were back competing at the showpiece event. The 1937 Grey Cup, played at Toronto's Varsity Stadium, was by no means a classic. The Toronto Argonauts triumphed with a 4-3 victory.

The following season it was the same two teams squaring off again for Canadian football's biggest prize. In front of a then record crowd of 18,778, Toronto used the home advantage to blow out their rivals from the West, 30-7.

On December 9, 1939, three months after Canada had declared war on Germany, Jeff Nicklin and the Winnipeg Blue Bombers appeared at their third consecutive Grey Cup, following an impressive 10-2 season.

They were back out east for the contest, this time against quarterback Orville Burke and his Ottawa Rough Riders. There were 11,738 inside Ottawa's Lansdowne Park. Conditions were not great. Temperatures were as low as minus five Celsius and the football field was covered with snow.

Winnipeg had another disadvantage in the game. At that time, Western rules allowed linemen to block ten yards past the line of scrimmage, while the East played under a three-yard rule. The Blue Bombers were forced to play under the Eastern standard. They had to adapt quickly.

There appeared to be no issues for Winnipeg though. Jeff Nicklin and the Bombers secured their second championship, with the star back having an influential role in the triumph. Towards the end of the game, with the contest heading to overtime, he recovered a kick that was intended for Ottawa's Orville Burke. Burke fluffed his lines and Nicklin pounced.

There are many differences between Canadian football and American football, such as Canadian football having 12 players per side on the field. It has three downs rather than four, and a 20-yard end zone instead of ten. The Canadian league also has the *rouge.* A rouge is a single point that is earned when the ball is kicked into the end zone, and the receiving team cannot return it.

Time was nearly up when Jeff Nicklin recovered that ball deep into Ottawa territory, and thus regained possession immediately for Winnipeg. It gave the Blue Bombers a couple of plays for Art Stevenson to kick the winning point. Winnipeg prevailed 8-7 in the freezing winter conditions at a stadium that was more than a thousand miles from home and their loyal support.

Nicklin was a four-time All-Pro and two-time Grey Cup champion. He was at the peak of his powers on the football field, having helped take the Winnipeg Blue Bombers to four championship games. Despite all his success as a professional sportsman, and before he could defend the latest title with his team, he hung up his cleats and enlisted on August 13, 1940, as a young officer with the Royal Winnipeg Rifles to serve his country in the Second World War. A few weeks later he married long-time girlfriend Mary Eileen Hollingsworth on September 14, later settling in Port Credit, Ontario.

* * *

During the early years of the war, airborne forces and parachute regiments were deemed a luxury that small nations such as Canada could not afford. But as the war rumbled on, American and British forces harnessed these divisions and worked on developing them in the belief that they innovated strategy and evolved combat. Therefore, in 1942, the Canadians decided to form their own battalion of paratroopers.

After its initial reluctance, the Canadian Army went all-out with its approach. The Parachute Battalion was given an elite status, with the Army commander declaring, 'Only the best men will do.'

The *Canadian Army Training Memorandum* made clear its expectations of the volunteers: 'Parachute training is tough,' it said. 'It needs young men, alert and clever young men, who can exploit a chance and who have the guts necessary to fight against overwhelming odds and win.'

This caught the eye of the extreme competitor, Jeff Nicklin, and so he signed up. Canadian football's young star was sent to Fort Benning in Georgia, where he would be put through intense training.

Senior commanders knew that the standards for paratroopers needed to be much higher than for an infantry soldier, and so the stamina and powers of endurance within the young volunteers were pushed to the limit. The Army declared that a strong emphasis was put on the theory, as well as the rigorous training. A screening process had been put in place, which graded the men from A (outstanding) to E (rejected). Only those who scored an A were kept for airborne training.

There were personality tests, word association tests and psychiatric questioning. Only half of those who signed up made it. The ones who did were described by the media as 'action-hungry and impatient to fill their role as the sharp, hardened tip of the Canadian army's "dagger pointed at the heart of Berlin"'. Jeff Nicklin was one of those who passed. The 28-year-old returned to Canada as deputy commanding officer and ruled with an iron fist as he put his battalion through intense training at Camp Shilo in the province of Manitoba.

It is often said that great players do not make good coaches. They struggle to conceal their frustrations when athletes with less talent fail to execute the things that they found so easy. This may have been an issue for Nicklin. He was an elite performer who achieved anything that he set his mind to. The former CFL All-Star wanted the same from his battalion. He was a notorious taskmaster. At training he would push his men to the limit from dawn until dusk and allowed little leave. His goal was to get them to their peak mental and physical performance, so when they were called into action, they would be ready to execute. Although he was tough, he would not push his battalion to do something that he could not do himself.

As well as the weapons training and sharpshooting, fitness was a priority. Every morning before breakfast, he would demand a two-mile run from each of his men. At times in the month, ten-mile runs in full battle gear with weapons had to be completed in less than two hours. He also enforced 50-mile marches throughout training.

In July 1943, before leaving Canada for England, the 1st Canadian Parachute Battalion was inspected by Major-General J.P. Mackenzie. The assessment of Mackenzie rated Nicklin as 'a good leader and, as a training officer, very satisfactory'.

In England he trained with the Sixth Airborne Division for several months in preparation for Operation Overlord. On June 6, 1944, Nicklin was one of the first Canadians to jump from a plane and into Normandy as part of the D-Day operations. He did this with a broken shoulder.

Speaking to the *Winnipeg Free Press* in 2007, Bill Jenkins, who served under Nicklin from the early training days in Shilo, shared his memories of the Normandy invasion. 'A week before D-Day, Jeff realised the troops had not been in battle before and they were uptight and worried about what was going to happen to them next week,' Jenkins said.

To help ease the tension, the two-time Grey Cup winner set up a football game. 'In the first play of the game,' Bill Jenkins recalled, 'Jeff took the ball and was making an end run. One of the sergeants, Ernie Appleton, who weighed about 140lb, had Jeff – at 220lb – coming at him. What was Ernie to do but drop down in front of Jeff? Jeff went flying through the air and landed on his shoulder and broke it.'

A few days later, complete with parachute, full military kit, including a 30kg (66lb) supply bag attached to his body, and broken shoulder, Jeff jumped into Normandy and the full force of German artillery.

His battalion's mission was to drop into enemy territory, seize villages from the Germans and hold them so that the beaches would be protected to allow the Allies to invade via the shore along the English Channel. Bridges within those villages would need to be destroyed, along with other German arteries, so that they could get to the beaches.

The drops did not go according to plan. There were poor navigational aids, plus a combination of heavy dust and smoke that drifted over the drop zones because of heavy bombing. Anti-aircraft fire panicked pilots into taking evasive action and resulted in paratroopers being scattered over a wide area.

Ross Munro, the *Canadian Press* war correspondent, reported that Jeff Nicklin landed alone, in the centre of the German-garrisoned town of Varaville. His parachute became entangled on the roof of a house and left him dangling down the side of the wall as the Germans scurried about the town. Nicklin was spotted and shot at by the enemy. He managed to cut himself loose and took cover. The running back who made a living from evading the force of the opposition worked his way from building to building with platoons of Germans stalking him. It took him an hour to get clear of the buildings and into the nearby fields, where he linked up with other Canadians.

Nicklin said, 'The Germans were really windy in Varaville.' His quotes were printed in a report for the *Winnipeg Evening Tribune*: 'They ran round that town like crazy men and shot at anything that moved. Even a moving cow would get a blast of machine-gun fire. They were so jumpy they ran around in twos or threes to give themselves moral support.'

Nicklin would continue to share the risks put on his men and visited soldiers in their forward positions, sometimes partaking in reconnaissance patrols. Just over six weeks after D-Day, he was seriously wounded. Whilst on patrol he tripped a wire and set off an improvised mine. Shrapnel hit him in the arms, legs, and buttocks. He was sent to hospital in England to recover.

In November 1944, he was promoted to lieutenant-colonel. He had been acting lieutenant-colonel since late September. His goal was to command the best battalion in the division. Battle-hardened paratroopers who put up with his intense training regimen before the war were increasingly reluctant to go through it again. Nicklin made an impression on the wave of new recruits landing in England, but not the veterans, many of whom went on hunger strike in protest.

One officer observed, 'Jeff Nicklin was one who almost seemed indestructible, six foot three inches tall, football hero back home, a stern disciplinarian, physical fitness his speciality.'

Nicklin fostered his Grey Cup-winning team mentality and used it along with the knowledge and experience he had learned from D-Day to help mould a battalion that operated on the battlefield like a football team on the gridiron.

A few days into the hunger strike, six paratroopers requested a meeting with the brigadier. Some of them owned up as the ringleaders of the protest. The brigadier heard their cases, and no disciplinary action was taken. On Christmas

Eve, Nicklin led the battalion into Belgium and the Battle of the Bulge. It was the biggest offensive of the war and the last major German military assault in western Europe, with more than a million men taking part from both sides.

A few months later the Germans were retreating, and the end of the war was in sight. Operation Varsity was launched on March 24, 1945. Involving more than 16,000 paratroopers and thousands of aircraft, it was the largest airborne operation in history to be conducted on a single day and in one location. The Allies were jumping into Germany, along the Rhine, with the goal of marching into Berlin.

Frederick Griffin, war correspondent for the *Toronto Star*, described Nicklin's fate in the Rhineland on that day: 'Jeff, in the lead plane of the flotilla carrying the 1st Canadian Parachute Battalion, was one of the first to jump and one of the first Canadians to die beyond the Rhine. This was his second operational jump in enemy territory. His first was into Normandy that June night before our invasion landings. When he floated to land this time, he caught on a tall tree and the Germans shot him hanging as he tried to get out of his chute.'

In an interview with the *Winnipeg Free Press* in 2007, Bill Jenkins recalled the tragic events of that day, 'I almost got sick on the spot. It was horrid. Even now, 60 years later, the 24th of March 1945 sticks out like it was yesterday,' Jenkins said.

He added, 'We were getting ready to cross the Rhine … most of us landed in a field. Jeff's chute was caught in the wind. It blew him into the trees bordering the dropping zone. I could see some enemy shooting at us, and I ran into the woods. Jeff was hanging in a tree riddled with bullets.'

Nicklin had been reported missing and rumours began to surface about his fate. In response to the rumours, the Canadian Army sent an investigative team to determine what had happened to him. The rumours were that he was killed by his own men out spite for the heavy discipline he enforced on them, but it was proven that his death was a result of enemy action.

Nicklin normally jumped in the middle of the stick so that he could have half of his squadron on either side of him upon landing. However, for this operation he wanted to be the number one jumper because he had planned to lead his troops into battle. He was 30 years old.

Jeff Nicklin was posthumously appointed an Officer of the Order of the British Empire.

He had a 15-month-old son whom he never met.

Steve Daniels, the former CFL head statistician perfectly summed up this gifted, heroic individual when he said, 'To just go off and volunteer like that while at the top of your professional sporting career, it is about as admirable as it is possible to be. And for me, if there is a gap in the Canadian Football League Hall of Fame, that gap revolves around the name of Jeff Nicklin. This is not based primarily on his skills, but I think on his character as well.'

As a tribute to their commander, the 1st Canadian Parachute Battalion donated the Jeff Nicklin Memorial Trophy to the Western Interprovincial Football Union in 1946. It was first awarded annually to the player in the West Division considered most valuable to his team. For the past 50 years, that honour has been awarded to the Most Outstanding Player in the West Division. Nicklin's name lives on through the sport that made him so beloved to many.

Jeff Nicklin is buried at Groesbeek Canadian War Cemetery, located five miles south-east of the town of Nijmegen and close to the German frontier.

CHAPTER 10

Tommy Thompson

'I always knew growing up that he was a great football player and he played for the Philadelphia Eagles'

– Sharon Early, Tommy Thompson's niece

THROUGHOUT NFL history, only 12 quarterbacks had won consecutive championships before the culmination of the 2023 season. Tom Brady was the last player to do it, winning back-to-back Super Bowls in 2004 and 2005.

Sid Luckman was the first to achieve the feat in 1940 and '41. The next quarterback to do it was Tommy Thompson with the Philadelphia Eagles in 1948 and '49. Not including Brady, all the other ten quarterbacks are in the Hall of Fame. Tommy Thompson is not. His 1949 championship ring is there – I have touched it. And it is only a matter of time until Brady is enshrined in Canton.

Until 1947, the Eagles had never made the playoffs. During that era, only the top team from each division qualified for the post-season, which was the Championship Game. The only exception would be when teams in the same division finished with an equal record, in which case, the right to represent their division would be contested in a playoff game between the two teams.

It only took Greasy Neale three seasons to build a winning team in Philadelphia, although that first winning season was with the Steagles. However, in the season following that one-off merger, Neale's Eagles began to take off.

They finished second in the East Division three seasons in a row from 1944 to 1946. Tommy Thompson returned from the war in '45 but Roy Zimmerman had led them to their first seven-win season the year before and was the starter for the campaign. Philadelphia won seven games again in 1945, just one behind division winners, the Washington Redskins.

It was 1947, with Zimmerman in Detroit, when Thompson was handed the reins of Neale's offence. The man who had been involved in the Allies' second Normandy landing in 1944 was displaying his leadership skills on the football field, guiding the Philadelphia Eagles to their first ever division crown. They did it the hard way.

Tied with a similar 8-4 record, the Eagles faced the Pittsburgh Steelers in an East Division playoff for a place in the Championship Game. The Eagles travelled across the state to a Forbes Field packed with almost 36,000 fans and silenced the crowd with a 21-0 victory. Thompson threw for 131 yards and two touchdowns.

Despite throwing for 297 yards and a touchdown in the Championship Game, Thompson was picked off three times and the Eagles' wings were clipped by the Chicago Cardinals in a 28-21 defeat.

From 1947 through the two championship seasons of '48 and '49, Thompson threw for a total of 5,372 yards and 57 touchdowns. He had the highest passer rating of the entire league in 1948 and 1949. 'Tommy Thompson kind of was that ultimate throwback player as we would call him today,' Joe Horrigan, the former executive director of the Pro Football Hall of Fame, told me when I visited the museum in Canton, Ohio.

'He was a triple-threat quarterback, who had excellent running ability, as well as being a very good passer,' Horrigan added. 'In Philadelphia, he's still revered as one of the greats of the team. And unfortunately for him, he's not yet in the Pro Football Hall of Fame. He has been nominated; he has been a candidate. But he's one of those guys that somehow history has not been particularly kind to in the sense of remembering him.'

Thompson was an undrafted free agent out of the University of Tulsa in 1940. The Pittsburgh Steelers picked him up and gave him his first shot. He played in 11 games in his rookie year, although he only started two as the Steelers went 2-7-2. The following year he moved to the Eagles.

Standing at 6ft 1in, and weighing 192lb, Thompson was very much your quintessential all-American. But what made his football and army careers even more remarkable was that he was legally blind in one eye. As Joe Horrigan said, 'It sounds like a bad joke when you say your quarterback is blind, right? But he actually was, which is incredible when you think about it. Here is a quarterback who won two NFL titles with one eye. It was a handicap that he clearly overcame.' 'The story goes that he was probably around eight years old,' Sharon Early, Thompson's niece told me, 'and he and his sister were playing outside, doing what kids do.

'They were tossing rocks and mud pies and anything they could find at each other,' Sharon added. 'And he took a hit to his left eye. And, as I understand it, this accident created a blood clot. Although he had minor vision in that eye, he was essentially blind, because everything he saw out of it was completely blurred.

'I found a book called *The Pro Quarterback*, I think it was printed in 1960. And the book refers to the fact that Tommy used to have to cock his head to the side when he stepped back to make a throw, so that he could see out of the good eye. And that always left his blind side wide open to being taken down. So that was always the story. I remember as a little kid being so proud of this. I would tell anybody I knew, and I still do actually, if I run into anybody who's interested in professional football, I talk about Tom.

'And that in itself speaks to the success as a passing quarterback in the National Football League. He had an outstanding passer rating with the Philadelphia Eagles and the T-formation throughout that era and he was handicapped with his vision.'

His niece still has vivid memories of watching her uncle play in the NFL. 'I always knew growing up that he was a great football player and he played for the Philadelphia Eagles,' she reminisced. 'The Eagles have always been my team because of that. I loved him as an uncle. He was the fun uncle. I just remember my dad, Tom's brother, talking about how there was some disappointment that Tom had not made it into the Pro Football Hall of Fame. He had actually been nominated for it on several occasions.

'I saw Tom play football in Dallas, Texas, when I was around four years old, so it probably would have been his last year. And I was very young at the time and the only thing I remember is that it was snowing and snowing in Dallas. I mean, my recollections of Tom were mostly post-football when he was really retired from the game. But this game stood out. I was so proud.'

In 2012, Tommy Thompson was inducted into the Philadelphia Sports Hall of Fame. To mark the occasion, *The Philadelphia Inquirer* spoke to a former team-mate from Thompson's illustrious Eagles days. Speaking to the *Inquirer*'s Frank Fitzpatrick, Bill Macrides, the backup quarterback on those title-winning Philadelphia Eagles teams, said, 'He was a good player. He always did the right thing on the field. The other guys recognised that and respected him.'

The *Inquirer*'s article, headlined 'Eagles great Tommy Thompson finally makes Phila. Sports Hall of Fame', published on November 8, 2012, featured an interview with the late Al Wistert, who said, 'I think the real key to those titles was Tommy Thompson. He had those indefinable qualities that make a player a winner.'

Much of the 1948 NFL Championship Game was focused on the rematch between the Eagles and Chicago Cardinals, who had beaten Philadelphia by a touchdown in the showpiece 12 months earlier. Thompson had been named second team All-Pro in the week leading up to the game. He had excelled in the T-formation that Greasy Neale had adopted, having studied the Chicago Bears' offence so closely. However, Neale would admit that nobody mastered the formation like George Halas. 'I've got a lot to learn,' Neale said.

Neale was a winner, and he knew he had a quarterback in Thompson that could deliver the National Football League title that had eluded him since he took the head coach job at Philadelphia in 1941. Nearly three decades before the 1948 Championship Game, he had won the World Series as a player for the Cincinnati Reds. He led the Reds with ten hits during that eight-game series. Neale also had a stint with the Philadelphia Phillies, but his main love was football.

In 1922, Neale coached the small college of Washington and Jefferson, surprising everyone as they went unbeaten and upset California with a tie at the Rose Bowl. He briefly returned to baseball and coached the St Louis Cardinals, but eventually went back to the gridiron.

The 1948 NFL Championship Game was played at Philadelphia's Shibe Park. There was a buzz among the home crowd after the previous year's finale had given the Eagles a huge disadvantage as the road team. There was heavy snowfall around Philadelphia on December 19, 1948. Cars were stuck on inclines and ultimately abandoned as eager fans flocked to the stadium. Nearly 29,000 braved the elements, determined to see the Eagles finally clinch the NFL title.

There was four inches of snow, and Burton Hawkins reported in the *Washington Evening Star*, that people were eagerly trying to make what they could from ticket sales. One scalper was heard saying, 'Two together for a dollar apiece.' The original value of the tickets was $5.25 each. Hawkins added that a few steps away a youngster was pleading for just 50 cents per ticket. Although 29,000 were inside the stadium, 38,000 tickets had been sold before the weather turned.

The snow was so thick and heavy that both teams were led out to help move the tarpaulin. More than one hundred men struggled to shift it in time for kick-off. Indeed, the game was delayed by 25 minutes because the tarpaulin would not budge. Shovels were needed to remove the snow and present some form of playing surface. It was the first time ever that a day game was played with the lights on.

Fans who had hoped to experience an epic tussle between the National Football League's two top teams were left disappointed. The conditions did not do any favours for the spectacle. It was a chess match between the opposing linemen. Backs struggled to run with the ball and the passing game was virtually non-existent. Efforts were made to keep the players comfortable in the conditions. Heat pads were rushed on to the field during time outs, hands were kept warm whenever possible, but the inevitable fumbles occurred. It was a fumble that ultimately won the game for Philadelphia.

The Chicago Cardinals' Ray Mallouf dropped the ball deep in his team's own territory and it was swiftly recovered by the Eagles' Frank Kilroy. It took the next four plays for Philadelphia's Steve Van Buren, that season's league rushing leader (945 yards), to stomp his way into the end zone for the score. Players had to dig in the snow and clear a patch of field for the resulting extra point. The kick was good, and the Philadelphia Eagles won 7-0.

The *Washington Evening Star* had the subheading 'Thompson Stars as General' over its report of the game. Van Buren had rushed for 98 yards in the contest, but Tommy Thompson also ran for 50 yards. The game report said, 'All of Thompson's gains were short thrusts through the line, but several were good for important first downs. One such strike preceded Van Buren's touchdown plunge in the fourth period on the five-yard line.'

Thompson displayed astute handling, despite the conditions. He had thrown a 65-yard touchdown pass in the heavy snow, but it was called back for a false start. With Neale at the helm and Thompson backed up by powerful runner Van Buren, it was anticipated that the Philadelphia Eagles were building a dynasty in the City of Brotherly Love. Thompson led the league with 25 touchdown passes in 1948.

They did not disappoint in 1949, marching to the Championship game with an 11-1 record. The Eagles were the only team to have double-digit wins that season. Van Buren led the league in rushing again, with 1,146 yards on the ground. Their opposition for the title that season were the 8-2-2 Los Angeles Rams. The Rams had moved from Cleveland to LA in 1946.

The 1949 Championship Game was played at the Memorial Coliseum in California, so there was no risk of heavy snowfall affecting the contest like the previous year. Leading up to the game, the Eagles were heavy favourites to win. They had beaten the Rams 38-14 in Philadelphia six weeks before the finale. It was reported that Neale's Eagles were handicapped as the seven-and-a-half-point favourites for the contest. The reigning champions were the most balanced team in the National Football League throughout that season.

There was no California sunshine on December 18, 1949, however. The rain was so bad that officials from both teams were willing to postpone the game until after Christmas. Bert Bell, the NFL commissioner, refused to switch it. He was 2,700 miles away in Philadelphia when he made the call.

The downpour persisted and even two layers of tarpaulin could not keep the field dry. Once again, the National Football League's flagship event fell foul of the elements. A crowd of 70,000 was anticipated in the days leading up to the contest, but only 22,000 braved the rain. There was little passing; instead it was another bruising battle in the trenches, with players slipping about on the mud.

Tommy Thompson threw a 31-yard touchdown pass to Pete Pihos to open the scoring in the second quarter. A blocked punt return in the third quarter doubled the Eagles' lead. They won 14-0 and claimed their second consecutive title. Steve Van Buren ran for 196 yards. The Rams did not make a single first down from a running play throughout the entire game.

Thompson and Neale continued with the Eagles for one more season. They struggled to a 6-6 record; Thompson threw for a total of 1,680 yards, 11 touchdowns and 22 interceptions. Thompson played nine seasons for the Philadelphia Eagles and Pittsburgh Steelers. He threw for 10,385 yards and 91 touchdowns. By the time he retired from the National Football League in 1950, Thompson was only the fourth person in history to throw for more than 10,000 yards. The others were Hall of Fame quarterbacks, Sid Luckman, Sammy Baugh, and Otto Graham.

When Greasy Neale was inducted into the Pro Football Hall of Fame in 1969, he said, 'I was the first man in the National Football League outside of [George] Halas that ever used the T-formation. I couldn't make it go, so I spread it out, put a man in motion, and came back on the end. And

Jimmy Castiglia ran, he must have run for 100 touchdowns, over 40 yards that year [1941].'

Neale added, 'The people in the stands said we ran the T-formation better than the Bears did. We won the Eastern championship three times, and we won two National championships, 1948 and 1949.'

At the end of Neale's second season, in 1942, Thompson was drafted to fight in the Second World War. He was 24 years old when his professional football career was put on hold, and he subsequently headed off to Europe to serve his country.

Thompson was based in England and became a sergeant in the United States Army infantry division. During the Allies' second Normandy landing, the Philadelphia Eagles' quarterback was wounded in action. He later received a Purple Heart.

His retirement at the end of the 1950 season took a lot of people by surprise. He was 32 years old when he hung up his cleats with the Eagles and took up an assistant coaching job at the University of Arkansas at Fayetteville. A few years later he was offered a coaching job in the CFL with the Winnipeg Blue Bombers.

Whilst serving as their backfield coach, Thompson made a few brief appearances at quarterback. Their new stadium had opened the year he arrived, and Thompson threw the first ever touchdown pass in the new home. The stadium stood for 60 years until it was demolished in 2013.

The former NFL champion played twice more, as his beaten body struggled with the rigours of the sport. At the end of the 1953 Canadian Football League season, he retired for good.

Thompson had a year as backup coach at the Chicago Cardinals and spent two years with the Calgary Stampeders as an assistant. When Calgary fired their head coach, Jack

Hennemier, in September 1956, Thompson had already been offered the job but declined it.

Tommy suffered from ill health and was confined to a wheelchair in the early 1970s due to severe arthritis. In the final 12 months of his life, he fought a brain tumour. During that period, he returned to Philadelphia to mark the 40th anniversary of his Eagles team's title success.

Tommy Thompson died on April 25, 1989. He was 71.

CHAPTER 11

Paul 'Pappy' Rowe

'He was a legend of his time who went off and served for his country'

– Steve Daniel, former CFL head statistician

OF ALL the football stars who played in the Tea Bowl and Coffee Bowl at White City Stadium, London in 1944, Paul 'Pappy' Rowe was the only one to have been honoured by his league in their Hall of Fame. As Bill Powers wrote for the Calgary Stampeders' website, 'Rowe's fame lasted far beyond his years on the field and in life.'

Born in Victoria, on Vancouver Island, British Columbia, Rowe excelled at sport from a young age. He played rugby, cricket and consistently won at track and field. Paul's son, Robert Arthur Grey Rowe, wrote his father's biography. *The Life Story of Canadian Hall of Fame Great Paul Rowe* provides an in-depth and heart-warming account of Pappy's life. In it there is a photograph of a 13-year-old Paul Rowe running in a track event and at that age he had a body that was toned and developed beyond his years. The boys competing against him had no chance.

That athletic build and desire to win took him to greatness in his professional sports career. It was a career that was put on hold for the war, but he returned, and became a hero to thousands. He has been immortalised in multiple

Halls of Fame, including the Canadian Football League's and the Canadian Sports Hall of Fame.

During 1935/36, the New Zealand All Blacks toured Great Britain, Ireland, and Canada. Their tour ended on the Pacific Coast, where they played two games in Vancouver and Victoria. Rowe, a winner of British Columbia's rugby competition, the McKechnie Cups in 1936, had been selected to play against the mighty All Blacks. He was 15 years old. Canada had a young sports star in its possession.

Rowe headed south of the border for college. Soon after his dominant displays on the rugby field, he swapped one oval-shaped ball for another. Little did he know that his path to football stardom was being paved.

The University of Oregon recruited him. After only his second year of playing football, Rowe was made honourable mention All-American. Perhaps it was his rugby training, but he had the speed and strength to break tackles and run through people on the gridiron. He was chosen ahead of more than a dozen young football stars to represent the famous Oregon Ducks at fullback.

This was an era when players had to operate on both sides of the ball, and Rowe did not let up on defence. He played linebacker and tackled as fast and as hard as he ran with the ball in his hands.

In his biography, Robert Arthur Grey Rowe wrote that the former Oregon All-American and Chicago Bears standout Mike Mikulak had described Paul Rowe as 'One of the finest running backs in college today, perhaps the finest in the country.'

Rowe did not see out college. Unfortunately for the young man, he ran out of money and his parents could not afford to fund him. The university tried to work out a scholarship, but professional football came calling. The Calgary Bronks had offered him a chance to continue playing, and, better still, he would be paid for it. The opportunity was too good to refuse. It was 1938 and he was heading home to Canada, where he would compete in the Western Inter-provincial Football Union.

There was another star back in the division at that time. Jeff Nicklin, whom Rowe would play alongside six years later in London, England, was powering the Bronks' rivals, Winnipeg, to multiple Grey Cup appearances.

'Paul Rowe was immediately one of the stars of the league in 1938,' said Steve Daniel, the former head statistician for the CFL. In his first season, Rowe had helped guide the Bronks to the Western final. Calgary faced Nicklin's Winnipeg in a best-of-two-game series. Winnipeg won and advanced to the Grey Cup, where they lost to Toronto.

'Rowe had a great record in 1939,' Steve Daniel added. 'He scored a remarkable 62 points that season. That's a lot of points.' Rowe was quickly making a name for himself in Canadian football. His natural sporting ability saw him dominate defences, en route to being awarded the league's scoring title.

'He was the Doug Flutie or Bo Levi Mitchell [Calgary Stampeders' two-time Grey Cup-winning quarterback] of his day,' said Daniel. 'Everyone recognised Pappy Rowe and made sure they got to games when he was in town, so that they could see him in action.'

When Canada declared war on Germany in 1939, Rowe, like so many young men, signed up for duty. The Calgary Bronks' 4-4 season in 1940 was hindered by absent players during practice. Rowe was one of those absentees. Military priority meant he was unable to participate in some of the training duties with his football team.

He was, however, granted time to marry Vivian. Soon after they exchanged vows, Rowe was sent to England where he would prepare for combat on the European front.

Rowe had been assigned a position with an anti-aircraft battery, where he would eventually be given the rank of captain. Like his fellow Canadian football star, Denis Whitaker, he took part in the tragic Dieppe raid on August 19, 1942. His landing craft suffered engine failure, which left Paul and his crew stranded offshore. This may have been a blessing, given what occurred on that disastrous day. A good friend, and many other men he knew, died during that raid. The football star was left to mourn the loss of so many.

The casualties he witnessed, along with his experiences of the bombing raids by German aircraft, fuelled Rowe with a desire for revenge and made him even more determined to punish his enemy. Perhaps this was the champion spirit that had made him gifted as a sportsman, or it may have been the hurt he had suffered since leaving his new wife and all he knew and loved at such a young age.

In letters to his wife, Paul wrote about bombs from the blitz landing 30 yards from his bed and described the devastation those raids had caused. He revealed how he encountered hundreds of elderly people and children sleeping on nothing but solid concrete in the bowels of the city of London, using the Underground stations and platforms as their refuge from the heavy bombardments above.

Rowe had shared in his letters to Vivian that he had become even more convinced that he was fighting for the right cause, and that he longed for the day to make the enemy pay for what they had done to the lives of the British families he was sharing these experiences with. As if he was being handed the ball on the gridiron, knowing that his team needed an explosive run from him, Rowe remained steadfast with his objective.

Whilst fighting abroad, Paul received news that his father had died. It was June 1942. In a letter to his two brothers, Rowe wrote about becoming the men that would make their father proud. He suggested that they make themselves worthy sons and be there to support their mother. There was a sense of accountability in his writing, telling his grieving siblings to keep their chins up. It was like stepping into a huddle after a punishing drive and telling his team-mates to give it an extra push to move the ball and show no weakness to the opponent.

He clearly cared for his family, but showed a paternal instinct to help them in the only way he knew how. To achieve the athletic success that he had, Rowe needed to have a clear focus and channelled his emotions to do what he believed was right.

Paul Rowe was involved in the Normandy invasion. The captain made the crossing in July 1944. He spent the next few months fighting in France, the Netherlands, Belgium, and later Germany. He was severely injured in May 1945. A German shell had wounded his body in 12 places. Men near to Rowe had been killed by the bombardment. He was extremely fortunate to survive. When he tried to stand, he couldn't. There were wounds to his legs and midsection. He was sent to hospital for weeks of recovery and finally retired from active combat.

Back home, Rowe was determined to return to normal. Some of that sense of normality came from football. In January 1945 the Calgary Stampeders had been formed. Although the Canadian football star of 1939 was five years older and battle-scarred, they signed him to their roster.

He did not play in that first regular season, but he did feature in their playoff games. The fullback showed his ability as a kicker, making the franchise's first ever field goal. History was being made by this future Hall of Famer. The Stampeders advanced to face the Winnipeg Blue Bombers for a place in the Grey Cup. Despite leading, Calgary were edged out by Winnipeg. The Bombers would lose that season's showpiece to the Toronto Argonauts, 35-0.

It was not long before Rowe found his feet in professional football. The 1946 campaign was the Stampeders' first full regular season. He was voted All-Star that season as the Stampeders finished 5-3, a record that earned them the top position in the Western Interprovincial Football Union. Winnipeg had also finished with a 5-3 record and faced Calgary in the two-game playoff series, from which the team with the best aggregate score would advance to the season finale.

The first game was played in Calgary and the Stampeders won 21-18. Could the mighty Blue Bombers finally be knocked off their perch in the West? They were the bullies of the division and had dominated it for years. With their backs against the wall, and a rabid fan base cheering every run, hit and tackle, the Blue Bombers shut out Rowe's Stampeders 12-0 and marched to Toronto, where they were beaten again by the Argonauts, 28-6.

Calgary held their home opener of the 1947 season against Winnipeg. Paul Rowe scored a touchdown in the 13-11 defeat. The Stampeders ended that campaign in second position in the West. Once again, Rowe was included in the Western All-Stars.

Déjà vu occurred again, as Calgary lost the two-game playoff to Winnipeg, only for the Blue Bombers to be defeated in the Grey Cup by the dominant Toronto Argonauts.

Success finally came to Rowe and the Stampeders. Led by their dynamic fullback, they went 12-0 in the 1948 regular season and marched to their first ever Grey Cup appearance. Rowe was so revered by the Calgary natives that the club honoured him in Week 9 of that '48 season with Paul Rowe Day.

In a way only Paul Rowe knew, he kept his composure throughout the fanfare and put on another scintillating display. That rare talent and instinct to win, a trait we have witnessed throughout the Tom Brady era of the NFL, ensured Rowe was locked onto his ultimate goal, which came a few weeks later.

'Paul really was an elite back, and he was a Canadian,' Steve Daniel said. 'That is a position that has long been dominated by what we call international players, basically Americans.'

Most of the guys that basically do most of the ball carrying,' Steve added. 'If you're looking for a soccer equivalent, he would be what Mohamed Salah has been to Liverpool Football Club. He is that guy you give the ball to because he's the most likely to score you some points.

'Paul Rowe was that player the Calgary Stampeders could rely on to score a touchdown if the ball was put in his hands.'

Everything Rowe touched in 1948 turned into gold. The flashy fullback was simply unstoppable. He led the league in scoring for the second time in his career and scored a touchdown against the Regina Roughriders in Game 2 of the WIFU Finals in Calgary. Their stadium was packed out with 10,000 fans who went delirious as their captain helped punch the Stampeders' ticket to the Grey Cup.

Perhaps fittingly, the game was played on Remembrance Day. Rowe was presented with the N.J. (Piffles) Taylor memorial trophy, which was handed to the Western champions. Even more poignant was that on the very same day, during the very same ceremony, the Jeff Nicklin memorial trophy for the West's outstanding player was presented to Rowe's team-mate, quarterback, Keith Spaith. Four and a half years earlier, Rowe had played alongside Nicklin on the gridiron in a stadium that was halfway around the world. That had been a day which brought respite and a brief moment of joy at a time when they desperately needed it.

Nicklin, a brother on that field in London, had tragically been killed in battle so close to the end of the Second World War, a man who would have been a star alongside Rowe in the Canadian Football League, had he survived: Jeff Nicklin, who never met his son. The trophy in honour of his name was being handed to the man stood by Paul Rowe's side. It was November 11. One can only imagine the emotions he must have felt. Rowe had ended a drought of sporting success for his adopted city, the crowd was raucous, and he was suddenly hit with the memory of a fallen friend, teammate, and comrade.

A column in the *Winnipeg Free Press*, titled 'Time Out with Maurice Smith', reported on Calgary's win over Regina. 'There didn't appear to be much doubt about Calgary Stampeders' superiority over Saskatchewan Roughriders yesterday,' Smith wrote. 'You knew the final result would be a Calgary victory. [Head coach] Les Lear and his boys, as has been the case all season, had too much power, too much reserve strength for the Riders as they gave the "Cow Town" its first Western grid championship in 37 years.'

Reports from the end of that season were unanimous in their conclusions that the unbeaten Stampeders were deserving of their place in the Grey Cup. 'All during the season they left little doubt in the minds of Western football fans that they were by far the best team on the prairies – perhaps one of the best ever,' reported the *Winnipeg Free Press.* 'Frankly it would have been a shame had the Riders upset the dope bucket and earned that berth in the Grey Cup final.'

Two weeks later, they would take on the Ottawa Rough Riders for Canada's top football prize. Paul Rowe was on the cusp of history.

The 1948 Grey Cup was played at Varsity Stadium in Toronto on November 27. It was the day Paul Rowe was christened with the nickname 'Pappy'. With Paul more than 2,000 miles away preparing for the biggest game of his life, his wife, Vivian, was giving birth to their second son, Robert. It also happened to be their first born, Barry's second birthday. The title was written in the stars for Rowe and his young family.

Robert Arthur Grey Rowe wrote in his father's biography that a slogan was going around Toronto, 'Win the Grey Cup for Pappy!'

Ottawa had been favourites heading into the final. There were 20,000 spectators inside the stadium. The Rough Riders got off to a fast start from the kick-off, but Calgary's defence kept them at bay. Before half-time, quarterback Keith Spaith threw a pass to Stampeder receiver Normie Hill. Hill caught the ball near the hashmark at the five-yard line. He was hit and the ball went loose into the air. Somehow, as he was falling on to his back, Hill managed to retrieve it and crossed the line for a touchdown. Calgary led at the break 6-1.

In the third quarter, the Rough Riders took a 7-6 lead, which they held heading into the final period. The Stampeders' defence stood firm and eventually their offence got another drive going. This time they got the score and sealed a famous 12-7 win. Paul Rowe and the Calgary Stampeders were champions.

Members of the team insisted that Paul's infant baby be named 'Grey Cup Rowe'. That is why he was christened Robert Arthur Grey Rowe. His father would forever be recognised as 'Pappy'.

The defending champions went 13-1 the following season and returned to the Grey Cup. Again, it was at Varsity Stadium in Toronto, but this time it ended in disappointment. The Montreal Alouettes proved too strong and had a 17-7 lead at half-time. There was little the Stampeders could do and they relinquished their title with a crushing 28-15 loss. Calgary would not win the Grey Cup again for another 22 years.

Following the 1949 season, Paul Rowe announced his retirement. He was lured back for a handful of games in

1950, but then hung up his cleats for good. He had achieved everything he wanted in the sport. We are left to ask what could have been had he not been forced to give up his prime years to the war. One of his team-mates had once described Rowe as an Adonis. He was a physical specimen at the peak of his powers. The Canadian Army and Calgary football clubs were lucky to have him.

For the first few years after retirement, Rowe had many business ventures. Unfortunately, he did not have the business acumen needed to run them successfully. As time went by, he lost his Adonis-like features and slowly became a shadow of the sports star who was marvelled at by thousands of loyal fans.

Racked with debt, he found solace in drinking. Alcoholism consumed him as his arrears grew larger. Friendships were broken and, after 29 years, his marriage ended.

Rowe, the superstar fullback who once bounced off tackles on his way into the end zone, had a life bouncing from place to place, trying to keep a roof over his head. The heavy drinking and smoking caught up with him. His stomach and kidneys were a wreck, and he was diagnosed with throat cancer.

It was a sad and tragic end to a life that had so many heroic moments. His twenties, especially those years pre- and post-war, gave him the life that millions would dream of. Without football he was a lost soul.

Paul Rowe died on August 18, 1990. The jersey he proudly wore at the Tea Bowl game in London on February 13, 1944, is on display at the Canadian Sports Hall of Fame in Calgary, Alberta.

CHAPTER 12

The Small Town With Big Heroes

'We're a border city, which has its own complexity to it'

– Michael Bradley, Mayor of Sarnia since 1988

APPROXIMATELY 265 metres of water separate Canada and the USA at the end of the Canadian westbound Highway 402.

On the east bank of the St Clair River is the city of Sarnia, Ontario. It currently has a population of around 72,000 people, making it the largest city on Lake Huron.

On the opposite bank is Port Huron, Michigan. A large steel-structured bridge dominates the skyline on Sarnia's waterfront, the Bluewater Bridge. The twin-span international bridge links the American Midwest with Toronto and the states of the north-eastern USA.

The Canadian city was built on industry. It grew because of its steelworks. 'We're not an old city,' Michael Bradley told me. Indeed, Sarnia only became a city in 1914. Michael has been Sarnia's mayor since 1988. He featured in the 2002 Michael Moore documentary film *Bowling for Columbine.*

'We're a border city, which has its own complexity to it. I'm here as the mayor and have been for more than 30 years. I was an immigrant, I came from Australia, my parents were from Northern Ireland.

'It's always been an industrial city. And one of the great achievements over the years was in the community, because of our isolation where we were back in the 1930s and 1940s, the development of sports really started to grow the character of the area and its people.'

The city has grown substantially since two of its sons played a football game in London, England (London Ontario is 62 miles east along Highway 402). Only 15,000 people lived in Sarnia during the 1930s and '40s. Petroleum became the main industry. Imperial Oil were the largest employers, and they would try and entice the best sports stars to the area with the promise of a decent salary, while allowing athletes to compete in the top competitions. The Great Depression had hit, therefore the financial power they pulled had allowed them to flex their muscles while other teams struggled.

'And that's why the Sarnia Imperials was formed,' Mayor Bradley explained. The team was established in 1928 and competed in the Ontario Rugby Football Union (ORFU). It was a good team. The Imperials got their name from the oil company and were nicknamed the Imps. They finished first in their division in their maiden season. The Imps only missed the playoffs once in their first 12 years.

'The industry bosses were the reason why so many great athletes came from this small community,' Bradley said. 'If you were a skilled athlete, the local oil company would hire you. You were not hired because of your skills as a pipe fitter, or a carpenter or whatever, but because of your skills as an athlete. In those days Sarnia was known for its industry and its championship-winning teams.'

The Imperials certainly stood out. Their blue jerseys had three bright red stars across the chest. It was an iconic look at a time of great austerity. Indeed, the Imperials had three Grey Cup appearances between 1933 and 1936. The city even hosted the showpiece in 1933, although the local team lost to the Toronto Argonauts 4-3. What is even more impressive is that this town of 15,000 was hosting a major event against an Argonauts team from Canada's metropolis, which had a population of well over 800,000 people. The minnows, albeit with a financial boost that most teams could only dream of at that time, were punching with the big boys.

As Mayor Bradley said, 'Sarnia in those days was well known for winning Grey Cups, which is the Super Bowl of sports today. Its football was incredible, and that was because of the calibre of the athletes that were brought to the area.'

The Sarnia Imperials brushed aside their Grey Cup disappointment of 1933 and went undefeated the following season. The Imps' running back, Norm Perry, won the ORFU's Player of the Year award in 1934 with his blistering runs and scoring ability. He and the Imperials made it back to the final, this time facing the Regina Roughriders from the West. Sarnia won the contest, which was held in Toronto, 20-12. Regina had been Western champions for eight of the previous nine seasons. Sarnia remains the smallest city to win the Grey Cup.

In 1935 they failed to successfully defend their crown, falling short in the playoffs. However, success followed in 1936. Determined to prove to the country that the title they won in 1934 was not a blip in the Canadian football archives, the Imperials marched their way back to Toronto for the showpiece. It was the Ottawa Rough Riders who stood between Sarnia and the trophy. The Imps overcame the team from the capital, winning 26-20. Sarnia never reached the Grey Cup again, but the name of the Imperials will forever be etched in history.

Players from Sarnia would be team-mates on a field in England more than seven years after that last Grey Cup success. Although neither were playing in those title-winning teams.

The Imperials disbanded during the Second World War. For the 1940 season the city still had a football team, the Sarnia 2/26 Battery, which existed for one year only. Their star centre was Nick Paithouski.

Nick studied engineering at Queen's University in Ontario. Throughout his time at Queen's he played college football for the Golden Gaels. Paithouski had played snap, which is now centre, and linebacker with the Queen's football team from 1936–39.

The Golden Gaels list Nick Paithouski as 'the dynamo of the team' on their Hall of Fame website. He was put on the juniors because he was considered small, and won the Junior MVP award in 1936.

Despite his size, Nick, like so many star players, had the traits of a champion and a natural desire to win, and more than proved his worth on the Golden Gaels. The 1939 Most Valuable Player award was presented to Paithouski. Not the quarterback, nor the star running back, but the centre. It was a reward for his hard work and outstanding ability on the football field.

Paithouski is so revered at the university that the faculty of engineering and applied science has an award in his honour. The Nick Paithouski Prize is presented to the graduating engineering student who has demonstrated the most consistent improvement in academic performance.

Nick was a Sarnia native and the son of Polish-Ukrainian immigrants. His coach from his final season at Queen's described him as one of the best. He said Paithouski was not one of the biggest players but was 'loaded with desire'.

That desire earned him an All-Star honour in his first season playing in the CFL. After his season with the Sarnia 2/26 Battery in 1940, he moved west and joined the Regina Roughriders. Regina finished second behind Winnipeg in the Western standings. The two battled it out over a three-game playoff series to determine who would advance to the 1941 Grey Cup. The Blue Bombers won all three contests and finished with an aggregate score of 32-22. Winnipeg would become that year's Grey Cup champions.

Paithouski enlisted for the war in 1942 and served with the Royal Canadian Engineers, mastering the skills he had developed at Queen's University, and headed to Europe.

Nick's brother, Michael, was already serving in the war with the Royal Canadian Naval Volunteer Reserve. He would escort ships in the North Atlantic and off the east coast of Canada. Michael Paithowski (he spelled his surname with a W, while the rest of the family used the U), joined the Navy in 1941.

Later in the war, he was serving on HMCS *Shawinigan*. The ship would escort ships across the stretch of water from Nova Scotia to Newfoundland. In 1942 a passenger ferry had been torpedoed while transporting innocent members of the public.

On November 24, 1944, the *Shawinigan* was conducting an anti-submarine patrol when it was hit by a torpedo. The ship sank and everyone on board her was killed. Michael Paithowski had been home on leave for a brief period before joining the *Shawinigan*. It was the only time he met his infant son.

Nick Paithouski was in Europe at the time of his brother's tragic death. Nick's role with the Royal Canadian Engineers did not involve much fighting. 'Basically, he was designing and building bridges,' Nick's daughter, Janet Baker, told me when I met her at her home in Sarnia. 'And he would build the bridges, and then they would be blown up. So, it just seemed like it was a perpetual thing,' Janet explained.

'I know he spent a lot of time in Holland and various places.'

Paithouski and the engineers would be sent out in advance of the front lines and build bridges in preparation for the Army's deployments. 'His life was not as difficult as some people that were in the frontline troops, who were fighting and shooting. He was a lot safer in that regard,' Janet said.

'When he first tried to play football, he was told that he wasn't big enough. My dad wasn't the tallest person; he was about five foot eight. He always had this incredible drive, so he wanted to prove those doubters wrong. That commitment, determination and drive served him well in life.'

Nick was a platoon leader in the war. Over a period of 45 days, he built 51 bridges in Belgium, France, Germany, and the Netherlands. His work under immense pressure was vital in the success of the war.

Lieutenant Paithouski's military service record was acknowledged with the presentation of the Bronze Star from US President Harry Truman, an honour bestowed on a very small number of non-American servicemen, for supplying bridging parts and equipment to Allied forces in north-west Europe.

Janet Baker told me that her father was mainly in Europe during his time serving. Therefore, Denis Whitaker and his Canadian team were very fortunate to have Nick Paithouski in London to play a football game. We can only imagine how special it must have felt for that group of servicemen to step aside from the extreme pressures they were facing and return to doing the thing that they loved, playing football. Sharing that experience with team-mates would have been equally exhilarating.

After the war, Nick played football for the Hamilton Wildcats, remaining in the middle of the offensive line for two seasons. His daughter mentioned that he worked at one of Hamilton's steel mills while he was playing football there.

Paithouski married and moved back to Sarnia to start a family. He had two children, Janet and Joseph. The family moved to Ottawa, where Nick had been given a job with the Canadian government's Department for Transport. He also spent time working for the Ministry of Defence.

During his later years, Nick Paithouski returned to Sarnia. 'My dad was fairly disciplined with his workouts. Even as he grew older, he did a set workout routine every day.' Nick died on September 15, 1985. He was 68.

* * *

Charles 'Hank' Living was another Sarnia football player who featured at White City Stadium, London, in 1944.

Charles was one of eight children. His sister, Viola, died at the age of five, just days before Charles's tenth birthday.

His father, Charles Senior, had fought in the First World War and was hospitalised on multiple occasions. Charles Snr had suffered from influenza, then spent two months recovering from a bullet wound in his hip, later battling gas poisoning.

Charles 'Hank' Living grew up in Michigan and excelled at sports. During his childhood, his father left the family and moved to Canada. Charles Junior enrolled into St Michael's College in Toronto and coached sport, while still finding time to compete.

He took up a job and worked at the Ford Motor Company in Detroit. After just over a year at Ford, Living returned to education at Michigan State.

Imperial Oil came calling after graduation in 1938. The Imps signed him up as their snap, the same centre position as Nick Paithouski. From the Sarnia Imperials, Living moved to the Eastern giants, the Toronto Argonauts.

Hank Living enlisted for the Royal Canadian Air Force in 1941. He wanted to be a pilot, therefore over the next twelve months he racked up his airtime and trained for his wings. In the summer of 1942 he received his Pilot's Flying Badge, having graduated as an above-average pilot with excellent airmanship.

Hank was not sent to Europe straight away. For nearly 18 months he continued his training. The football star had become so good, he was given the task of training others. During the spring of 1943, he married, and he and his new wife set up home in Sarnia. Later that year, in November, he was sent to England.

For a while he did not see combat. Hank's training continued overseas, despite his adept piloting skills.

One of his brothers headed to England a few months earlier. Private Frederick S. Living fought in the army, as his father had done during the Great War. Frederick entered France in July 1944. On August 6, as the Battle of Normandy continued to rage, Hank's 23-year-old brother was killed in action. Grief had struck the Living family once more, as though an evil curse had been cast over their name.

Hank Living became a member of Bomber Command, flying the famous Lancaster bombers on dangerous missions over Germany. Hank's missions were above Dortmund, Dresden, Munich, and many more industrial targets deep in enemy territory. He flew 20 successful missions.

Living was a big man. His height was 5ft 10in. He had a stocky frame and a build one would associate with a Canadian football or rugby player.

'He was a big man,' Tom Slater, historian and author of *The Sarnia War Remembrance Project* told me when I visited the city. 'As a matter of fact, the squad guys would kid him about his size,' Tom added.

'Because he was the biggest man of the squadron, one of his fears was that he wouldn't be able to escape out of the emergency hatch in case there was a problem. He was worried that the additional layers of parachute and life jacket would get him stuck in the plane.'

Another pilot from Hank Living's squadron was Frank Phripp. Years later, Frank was the author of the book *The RCAF at War*. In that book, he recalled the evening he encountered his fellow member of 576 Squadron, Hank Living, in sobs of tears.

'I had never seen a man cry, that was unthinkable among my Air Force friends,' Frank wrote. 'And if the idea had occurred to me, Hank Living was the last man I would have expected to be so broken up. Hank was undoubtedly the biggest guy on our squadron. He had used his size well when he played centre on the line for the Sarnia Imperials in the Ontario Rugby Football Union. He was known as "Hi" Living in 1938 when he starred in the final game with the Montreal Nationals that won the Imperials the ORFU championship. Yet there he was on his cot in a dim corner of our hut in Lincolnshire, England, and heaving uncontrollably.'

Charles explained that he was afraid to keep flying, and he was certain he was going to be killed. Charles was a flight lieutenant at this point, and, despite his worst fears, he stuck to his job and continued flying.

In the late winter of 1945, just over 12 months after Hank Living had played in the Tea Bowl, he took to the skies in his Lancaster for mission number 21. Again, it was a night mission. This time the objective was to attack Duisburg, Germany. It was a major operation involving 370 aircraft. The noise would have been deafening.

At some point between 11:30 and 11:45 on the night of February 21, 1945, Living's Lancaster disappeared near the Dutch–German border. According to eyewitness reports the plane crashed with extreme force and burst into flames. All the aircrew perished. Charles was 30 years old. Tragedy had struck the Living family once more.

Living's mother, Viola O'Day, later lost her youngest son in the Korean War. Charles William Living was a sergeant and had been wounded in action during March 1951. The 19-year-old Living recovered from his wounds and returned to action a few weeks later. In June of that year, he was killed. Half of Viola's offspring had died young. The pain and heartbreak that she and her family suffered is unimagineable.

* * *

Like thousands of other comrades stationed across the globe, Nick Paithouski and Charles Henry Living were two servicemen from the same small city who were sent to fight. Sadly, for Charles, he paid the ultimate sacrifice for his country. He was a very good football player who became an excellent pilot. The city of Sarnia will never forget them.

'You know, the war veterans, the war heroes,' Sarnia's mayor, Michael Bradley said, 'in the last few years, there has been a great renaissance of respect and admiration for what they accomplished. The local community has worked very hard to share the stories of these incredible individuals.'

A lot of the information is thanks to the exceptional work that has been done by their local historian, Tom Slater. His book, *The Sarnia War Remembrance Project*, offers in-depth accounts of the many Sarnians who fought and served in both world wars. Their bravery and remarkable stories will live on thanks to Tom.

Every village, town, and city takes huge pride in celebrating their local sports heroes. This is no different in Sarnia, Ontario. 'We're a very proud sports city,' Mayor Bradley told me. 'Many people here that went through our amateur sports programmes went on to great success as professional athletes. One of the most outstanding ones was the golfer, Mike Weir. Mike won The Masters [in 2003]. Both our community and the whole of Canada are still proud of that achievement to this day. But in the National Hockey League, in other areas of endeavour with sports, this community has always moved forward in supporting our athletes. And I always remember when I first became mayor about 35 years ago, I was told "If kids aren't throwing balls, they'll be throwing stones." And that has been a really good philosophy and that is a philosophy that the city has adopted over the years.

'When Mike Weir won The Masters, it was absolute pandemonium. I know my own phone was ringing off the hook with media requests. And citizens calling to share their pride at his achievement.'

Canada's elite sporting success that Sunday on April 13, 2003, was thanks to their society coming together to help one of its own. 'We felt like his achievement was also our achievement. You see, this city, when he first decided to become professional, the whole community came together to raise the money for him could so he could go on the road to be an athlete without worrying about paying for the hotels, and all the other expenses that come with being a professional athlete. So, we had a sense of ownership. And he was the first Canadian to win that prestigious golf event. It was just a stunning achievement for a Canadian who came from Sarnia.'

Tears of pride ran down Michael Bradley's face as he shared his memories of Weir's triumph, which was incredible for the whole community. Sarnia stands on the banks of the river and looks across to its American neighbours with dignity and honour. Mike Weir's success really was an achievement for the city. It was their moment to ghost across that water and show the Americans how great they are. The impressive war project that has been produced by Tom Slater shares an equal sense of pride for the Sarnia natives that many of its population have never met. Sarnia is the epitome of community, and the support they offer their own should be celebrated. One may argue that it stems from the time of Imperial Oil, when the local industry backed its athletes and sports teams to build a winning organisation and brought national titles in an era when bigger cities could not even contend with the mighty powerhouses from the Toronto metropolis.

CHAPTER 13

Basil F. Russ

'This is a man that worked hard, sometimes three jobs. He was all about family'

– Gina Bower, Basil Russ's daughter

THERE WAS one man who was not keen on the idea of representing his country at the Tea Bowl in 1944. Basil 'Ben' Russ simply did not want to perform in front of a huge crowd at such a large venue.

'He did not want to play that game,' said Ben's daughter, Gina Bower. 'His commander called him in to tell him that he'd been selected for the match-up, and he told them he was not interested,' Gina explained.

The commander knew he had to field as strong a team as possible and Ben was important to their success. A strong American performance against the Canadians would provide a shot in the arm for the morale of his troops. 'And the commander said, "Ben, I have called you here because you are one of the best players that we have got,"' said Gina.

Eventually Russ admitted to his commander that he was too shy. He had never played top-level football before, nor had he played in a stadium with 30,000-plus people in it. Ben Russ was a young man from Harrisburg, Pennsylvania. He had no experience of competing on a grand stage such as the game that he was being asked to prepare for. 'The highest level of sport that he played at was high school,' Gina told me. 'High school crowds were the biggest he had played in front of. There were some big games that he played in, but not on the level of 30,000 spectators.'

The commander's powers of persuasion must have been exceptional because he managed to convince Russ to take part. Soon the young man from central Pennsylvania was preparing for the biggest game of his life.

* * *

Ben was born Basil F. Russ on September 23, 1921. His mother, Amelia, had remarried. She was widowed with five children before she met Ben's father, Frank.

Amelia, a young single mother with so many hungry mouths to feed, was forced to put some of her children into an orphanage.

When she married Frank, he adopted all her offspring and reunited the family. The couple had seven children of their own, which eventually made them a Catholic household of 14.

The Russ clan were of Italian heritage. Family was everything to them, and that was a special trait that Ben carried with him throughout his life. Of his 11 siblings, five of them were older stepbrothers.

Their family home was in a part of Harrisburg called Shipoke, which stood near the bank of the Susquehanna River. The river meanders through the city and is up to a mile wide. This expanse of water on which Harrisburg was built had a special bond with Ben Russ throughout his life. Even in his final years when Ben was living with dementia, his affinity with the river remained.

When Russ was young, he and his friend would get up and row the width of the Susquehanna every day. After they had rowed shore to shore, they would swim to the opposite bank and back. 'My dad was ripped back in the day,' Gina quipped. 'He was very athletic.'

Ben Russ excelled at sports. He attended a Catholic school in the city and took part in most events. 'He did not compete in basketball because he didn't like how short the shorts were. He said it was because he was too shy to wear them,' Gina said. Even though Ben had an athletic figure that most people could only dream of, he would not play the sport he enjoyed because he did not have the confidence to show off his chiselled legs.

American football and track were Ben Russ's sports as a youngster. His brother, Johnny, hung a tire from a tree and would get Ben to throw the football through it repeatedly to help improve his passing accuracy. 'He would practise it religiously,' Gina told me. 'He would do it for hours and also run squat drills.

'I don't know how, but Dad would still do those squats when he was 70–80 years old. He was an animal.'

There were nuns at Ben's high school. They were not allowed to attend football games, but Russ knew some of them would be watching from the classroom windows. There was one particular nun that Ben liked, and he would tell her that he was going to score a touchdown for her, sometimes even three. Whenever he did, he would look up at the window from where she was watching and give her a nod.

The local press was aware of his talent as an aspiring halfback and quarterback and would include reports on the 'outstanding star' in their write-ups of Russ's high school games.

When Ben was approaching graduation, the world had changed. It was at war. And like so many young men at that time, he felt a sense of duty to serve his country. Russ enlisted and trained at the Mississippi Military Academy. Whilst stationed there he managed to continue playing football, but not as regularly as he did at school. He graduated from the academy in May 1943.

It had been a whirlwind couple of months for Russ following graduation. He married his sweetheart, Doris, in July of '43 and was then called into service just a few days after their wedding. The young couple would have known that his number was going to be called at any moment, but there still would have been an enormous sense of anxiety as he was shipped off across the Atlantic Ocean, with huge uncertainty over what could happen. So many of those young men aboard his ship had never left home, let alone their country before. The tension must have been unbearable.

The anxiety would have been equally high, if not more, for the Russ brothers' mother because four of his siblings were also on active duty. Amelia Russ had five sons serving in the Second World War – Frank, John, Pete, Marlon (AKA Tony) and Ben. Frank, Pete, and Tony were in the Army, and John was a US Coast Guard.

Ben served as a member of the Military Police and was stationed at Hyde Park, near Buckingham Palace and Piccadilly Circus in London. His tour did not get off to the best of starts. He had an unpleasant experience getting to England on board the *Queen Mary*. The crossing was rough, and Russ suffered from seasickness. For most of the voyage he had trouble keeping food down as the ship rose high on the waves and came crashing back down. He was even denied the luxury of fresh air because the conditions on deck were frozen and too dangerous with the ice.

When he arrived in England, the young man from Harrisburg suddenly found himself in the middle of one of the biggest cities in the world. The culture was completely different to what he had been used to. Gina told me a story about her father's first experience with fish and chips. Chips to him were potato crisps to British folk. This young 'redneck', Gina's words, ordered his food and was shocked at receiving 'French fries' with something in batter.

For years Ben enjoyed sharing that story with his family, but at the time it must have been an overwhelming period in his life. He had just been whisked away from his new wife, made to cross an ocean on a voyage that had made him ill, only to land in a foreign metropolis filled with quirks that were completely alien to him. He was a young person that had been brought up with a massive family support network. That family was no longer around for comfort and safety. The small town he was used to had gone, replaced by a huge city with bombs being dropped all around him. So, to order food and be given something he had not been expecting must have been devastating.

It was not just the culture that was making Ben homesick. 'He did not like the weather,' Gina said. 'He respected Britain, he respected the British people, but the weather was not his thing.' A lot of accounts from soldiers stationed in Britain reported on their dislike of the climate.

Gina said the bombing of London gave Ben claustrophobia. He struggled to breathe when he was forced into the bomb shelters. In later life he could not wear a high-collar shirt because it made him claustrophobic.

One night, during a bombing raid, a commander ordered him to take cover in a nearby building, and he refused because of his fear. He said he had a better chance of surviving in the middle of Hyde Park than inside a structure that could crumble on top of him. Russ and a few men lay in the middle of the park.

Ben Russ may have been shy, but that did not stop him from testing the Royal Guards. 'He liked the guards at Buckingham Palace,' said Gina. 'He tried to get them to laugh, but they would never do it. He also thought it would be funny to get them to smoke a cigarette, but they would never do that either.'

His brother, Tony, was not far away. Ben, the military police officer, had been called to a public house one evening to reprimand his half-sibling, who had become too intoxicated by the local ale and was somewhat scrappy. According to his niece, Tony was the wild child of the Russ brothers and did not settle down with a wife until he was in his 50s.

Pete Russ was involved in the Normandy invasion and returned home from the war relatively unscathed. The only Russ brother to suffer serious injuries was Frank. He was also serving in Europe and had been shot in the head. Miraculously, he survived and lived with a metal plate on his skull. This did not affect his functions and he lived for many years after.

Ben had opportunities to meet the Queen and perform sports in front of her, but he turned it down because of his insecurity. The commander who later encouraged him to play in front of the huge White City crowd for the Tea Bowl was clearly deserving of a medal.

The fact Ben was allowed to serve is something of a surprise to his daughter because, like Tommy Thompson, he was legally blind in one eye. Yet, just like Thompson, he threw an American football with a degree of accuracy.

As the war rolled on, Ben had formed friendships, but he longed for home. His wife had given birth to a son he'd never met. Eventually he did get back to Harrisburg and he remained as loyal a son, husband, father, and grandfather as you can get.

Family was everything to Ben Russ. He had a football scholarship at the University of Tennessee, but he turned it down so that he could care for his mother, who had become seriously ill after suffering a stroke. She was only in her 50s and died young not long after her illness had started.

Ben's daughter, Gina, later asked him if he ever regretted that decision to turn down the university scholarship.

Because he was such a gifted football player, he had the potential for an exceptional career with more money than he could imagine. Russ's answer was humble. He insisted that he would not have changed anything because he would never have had his six children: Fran, William 'Jake', Amelia, Renee, Janice, and Gina.

Ben's Catholic family was growing, so he took up employment at the local steel mill. His dad was working there, as were some of his brothers. To help support his expanding household, Ben Russ would work two or three jobs. No matter what, his family came first. 'He was just the best father,' said Gina.

Later he worked as a delivery driver and a janitor at the local Catholic school. When he retired from the distributing company, he worked on the docks for a trucking company.

His greatest legacy is his family. He grew up in an Italian household whose doors were always open. Family meant the world to him. When his granddaughter was born, he was with her almost every day. The shy kid from Harrisburg, Pennsylvania had travelled the world, seen royalty, and was given the opportunity to become a great American football player. To his family, he was great. The greatest father and grandfather.

Despite his reservations about playing in front of a large London crowd, his moment in the international spotlight did not disappoint.

CHAPTER 14

The Right Honourable George Hees

'George's service to his country was automatic'

– Deborah Grey, Canadian Member of Parliament

OUT OF all the stars who played in the Tea Bowl, George Hees may have been the most flamboyant.

His father was a lawyer, and his family had a strong tradition of public service. Hees was educated at Trinity College, a private boys' school in the town of Port Hope, Ontario. He studied further at the Royal Canadian Military College, University of Toronto, and Cambridge University in England. Sports were his passion. After education he began his professional career as a Toronto businessman and was also signed by the Toronto Argonauts as a linebacker.

He played football for three seasons, 1934, 1937 and 1938. In his final season he won the Grey Cup with the Argonauts. Hees also fancied himself as a pugilist. In 1933 he took to the boxing ring and fought the Canadian heavyweight champion, Bill Maich. Maich dismantled his challenger with ease at Maple Leaf Gardens in Toronto. Despite his brutal defeat, Hees was not deterred and later beat the boxing champion of the British Army.

With the outbreak of World War II in 1939, Hees chose to fight. He served in various capacities, eventually rising to the rank of major during his military career. His leadership qualities and dedication to the cause made him an inspiration to the men he led.

'George Hees was a glorious man,' recalled former Lieutenant-Colonel Charles Forbes. Charles was interviewed by the journalist Rod Mickleburgh for his book *Rare Courage, Veterans of the Second World War Remember,* which was published in 2005. The account can also be read on Rod Mickleburgh's website, *The Mickleblog.*

Forbes, along with Hees, was involved in a bloody battle between Canadian troops and German forces in the Netherlands during the autumn of 1944.

'I was a platoon commander,' said Forbes. 'And you are the one in closest contact with the enemy because you have to lead your men. You don't tell them to "go there". You say, "Follow me." That's the way we fought in the Canadian Army. We had no professionalism, but we were adventurers. We were go-getters. We were voyageurs. We were full of courage. I lift my hat to the guts of the Canadian soldier. A German officer said once, "I know why the Canadians fight so well. It is because their officers fight with them." By the end of October, we were tired. Really beat. We had been in battle in France, northern France, Belgium, and Holland. No rest since July.'

Forbes and Hees were about to lead a battle to take Walcheren Island. The island is off a causeway linking it to South Beveland. It was part of the Battle of the Scheldt in the north-west Europe campaign of the Second World War. This costly battle was the final fight for the liberation of Antwerp.

October 31 was a cold autumn day. The plan was to cross the Slooe Channel from South Beveland on to the island.

The causeway was a mile long and around 40 yards wide. It was a long stretch with little room for movement. The men were easy targets for anyone protecting the island.

The Canadians had planned to make a lightning assault on the island and stun the German forces. The mud flats on either side of the causeway were unpassable and when the tide was in, boats were unable to cross. It had to be the causeway.

In the late evening of October 31, Black Watch went forward and bombarded the dykes on the opposite end of the causeway. They used all kinds of ammunition, including mortars and anti-aircraft artillery. Black Watch got about halfway before they were met with the full force of German defences. There were heavy casualties.

B Company of the Calgary Highlanders attempted to advance but found that the entrance to the causeway was under heavy German fire. An anti-tank gun that shot at high velocity was firing down the length of the causeway. There was a crater in the middle of the passing, which became the first target for the advancing Canadians. If they could reach it, they would have cover in their progress.

It was into the morning of November 1 when D Company moved down the causeway, inching their way towards the German roadblock at the far end. Eventually it was seized, and the objective was secured by mid-morning. D Company had lost all its officers killed or wounded. With the battalion under duress and without a leader, a brigade major stepped up and volunteered to take over. That person was George Hees. Hees went on with an artillery forward observation officer as his second in command. The linebacker was taking charge of his defensive unit.

Hees was shot in the arm but stayed put. Lieutenant-Colonel Ross Ellis later praised the heroics of Hees, 'It took a lot of guts for a guy who had never been in action to go into a hellhole like that one.'

The Calgary Highlanders suffered 64 men killed, wounded, or missing during the Battle of Walcheren Causeway. The battle is still commemorated annually.

As a result of his injury, George Hees was repatriated to Canada and discharged. Upon his return, Hees became so appalled at the government's handling of overseas troop shortages, he decided to run as an opposition Conservative in 1945. He lost, but that was not the end of his career in public office.

Five years later he won election to the House of Commons of Canada in a by-election. He was a popular figure in parliament and made headlines in 1952 when he hit the campaign trail hard for an upcoming by-election. It was a crucial seat that he had become enthusiastic about securing for the Tory party. So enthusiastic in fact, he confidently declared that he would 'eat his shirt' if the Tory candidate he was campaigning for lost.

The Conservatives lost, as the Liberal candidate romped home with a sizeable margin of 1,500 votes. There was one question on everyone's lips: would George Hees eat his shirt? The MP was a man of his word. A special shirt was created by a confectioner. Hees ate a piece and shared the rest with the newly elected Liberal MP and a select group of others. It was a ceremony that was hosted on a platform in front of the local city hall.

Televisions were creeping more into people's homes at that time, and this public event had drawn more crowds and media interest than the election campaign itself. Hees had generated a national reputation as a fun-spirited politician that people could relate to, and he remained popular throughout his career.

That fun persona made headlines again in 1958, when Hees was the minister of transport. He attended the sod-cutting for Edmonton's new airport. However, rather than stomp his foot on a spade and cut up a clump of dirt, Hees had secretly taken lessons on how to drive a bulldozer and, with dignitaries' mouths wide open, he began the excavation by ploughing up a good 20 feet of ground.

In the early years of his political career, Hees was known for his dedication to the principles of conservatism. He was a staunch advocate for limited government intervention in the economy, a strong military, and free-market policies.

Throughout his tenure in parliament, Hees held several key positions. He served as the Minister of Trade and Commerce under Prime Minister John Diefenbaker from 1957 to 1963. During his time in this role, he played a significant part in shaping Canada's trade policies and promoting international trade agreements.

One of Hees's most notable achievements as the Minister of Trade and Commerce was his involvement in the negotiation of the Auto Pact, which significantly benefitted Canada's automotive industry. This agreement fostered the growth of the Canadian auto sector and established Canada as a major player in North American automobile production.

Throughout his political career, George Hees remained a respected figure in the Progressive Conservative Party. He ran for the leadership of the party in 1967, although he was not successful in securing the position.

Hees was best known as Minister of Veterans Affairs. Through his own personal exploits during the Second World War, he understood the needs of military veterans. With that he proudly advanced Canada's tradition of providing benefits and services for those who served. The Veterans Affairs portfolio was one that he passionately enjoyed and his crowning achievements were benefits for Canada Service Only Veterans and the Veterans Independence Program (VIP), both of which have had a significant, enduring impact on the well-being of military vets.

George Hees died in a Toronto rest home on June 11, 1996, less than a week before his 86th birthday. Members of Parliament paid tribute to the late Honourable George Hees at the House of Commons on his birthday, June 17.

'Mr Hees was a great sportsman,' said MP Louis Plamondon from Quebec. 'As well, he was one of the few politicians to have been a minister in two governments, 20 years apart. He was a minister under Diefenbaker and again in the last Mulroney government.'

Plamondon added, 'His work on behalf of war veterans is acknowledged in every Canadian Legion, as well as throughout the world. He has been held up often as an example of support, not only moral support but also concrete action, on behalf of veterans, and for gaining recognition of their true value to society.'

Deborah Grey from the Reform Party said, 'George's service to his country was automatic, whether it was serving the country during World War II or whether it was serving in the House as he did for nearly four decades.'

Grey continued, 'George Hees was first elected in a 1950 by-election and won every election from then on until his retirement in 1988 with the exception of the 1963 election. Imagine running and winning every single time. That is an amazing legacy in itself.'

Tributes continued for 20 minutes within the Commons. Half a dozen MPs paid their respects to the former linebacker who served his country in combat and public service. Bill Blaikie from the New Democratic Party gave this tribute, 'I had the opportunity to sit in the House of Commons with Mr Hees for nine years. I echo the comments of the Minister of National Defence that George Hees was a House of Commons man and someone who gave to this place and to those who came here as new members an appropriate sense of the responsibility.'

Blaikie said, 'When George Hees became the Minister of Veterans Affairs in 1985 my case work with respect to veterans affairs dropped just like that. As Minister of Veterans Affairs he must have told the bureaucrats in the civil service: "Clean up your act. I want you to give the benefit of the doubt to veterans. I do not want any more of this stalling and delaying." It made a real difference. Anybody who was a Member of Parliament could see it at that time. Your case load with respect to veterans affairs literally disappeared overnight when George Hees became the Minister of Veterans Affairs. I want to pay tribute to that particular element of his career.'

Private First Class Frank Dombrowski (left) of the United States and Major William Denis Whitaker (Canada), rival captains of the teams playing in the Canada–United States 'Tea Bowl' football game at White City Stadium, London, England, February 13, 1944. Library and Archives Canada/ Department of National Defence fonds/a150135

Jeff Nicklin (left) played for the Winnipeg Blue Bombers from 1934–1940, winning two Grey Cup titles. He scored the final touchdown of the Tea Bowl, as Canada beat USA 16-6. Royal Hamilton Light Infantry Museum

Lieutenant-Colonel G.F.P. Bradbrooke (left), Commanding Officer of the 1st Canadian Parachute Battalion, and his Deputy Commander, Major Jeff A. Nicklin, outside Battalion Headquarters, Carter Barracks, Bulford, England, January 1944. Library and Archives Canada/ Department of National Defence fonds/179151

Corporal Frank A. Fenton, of Sunbury, Pa., No. 13, is tackled after a slight gain in an American football match between two US Army service teams at White City Stadium, London May 7, 1943, for the benefit of British Red Cross.

Tommy Thompson, who starred in the Coffee Bowl rematch for the United States, quarterback of the Philadelphia Eagles football team in posed action, July 28, 1950.

Members of the Chicago Cardinals help to clear away the heavy snow -- which delayed the game by half an hour – before the 1948 NFL Championship Game, a 7-0 loss to the Philadelphia Eagles on December 19, 1948, at Shibe Park in Philadelphia, Pennsylvania.

Tommy Thompson's championship ring from 1948, the Philadelphia Eagles' first NFL title. Thompson's family donated his ring to the Pro Football Hall of Fame in Canton, Ohio

Ben (Basil) Russ, who was one of the star players for the United States team in their 16-6 loss to Canada at the Tea Bowl, recognised as an honorary captain at one of the last games his former high school played before moving to a new school in 2013

(Left) *Former player for the Steagles, a wartime combination of the Pittsburgh Steelers and the Philadelphia Eagles in 1943, Al Wistert, runs onto the field during a ceremony honouring the surviving players during half-time of the pre-season game between the Eagles and the Steelers in Pittsburgh on Saturday, August. 16, 2003.*

Arizona Cardinals safety Pat Tillman tackles San Diego Chargers rookie running back LaDainian Tomlinson during Arizona's 20-17 win at Qualcomm Stadium in San Diego, CA on November 25, 2001.

Denis Whitaker (centre), who became a brigadier-general, during one of his many encounters with Prince Philip, the Duke of Edinburgh

Anthony Wootton and former Frankfurt Galaxy general manager Oliver Luck in Frankfurt, Germany on the eve of the first ever NFL game in the city, November 2023

Anthony Wootton with the leading NFL sportswriter Peter King at the Kansas City Chiefs press conference in Frankfurt, Germany

Anthony Wootton on board the Kansas City Chiefs' ChampionShip with NFL commissioner Roger Goodell, November 4, 2023

The Tottenham Hotspur Stadium gets set to host the Jacksonville Jaguars vs. Buffalo Bills on October 8, 2023. The venue has been given the status of the official home to the NFL in the UK

NFL
JAGUARS VS BILLS
BILLS
2023 NFL LONDON GAMES
QTR 1 12:43 4TH & 1 BALL ON 40
JAGUARS VS BILLS
GO BILLS
BILLS

Bayern Munich's Allianz Arena hosted the first ever NFL regular season game in Germany when Tom Brady and the Tampa Bay Buccaneers played the Seattle Seahawks on November 13, 2022 in front of a crowd of 69,811

Eintracht Frankfurt's Deutsche Bank Park, which hosted two NFL games in 2023; the Miami Dolphins vs. Kansas City Chiefs on November 5, and Indianapolis Colts vs. New England Patriots on November 12

SECTION 3

How Gridiron Stopped the War

CHAPTER 15

Cheers to Football

'I'd played QB for the Hamilton Tigers for several years before I enlisted, and I knew a number of Canadians serving in Britain who had played pro or college football'

– Denis Whitaker

FOOTBALL GAMES had been played in England and abroad throughout the Second World War. As we have established, there were competitions, and their purpose was to provide motivation for young men who were otherwise bored.

By the time Denis Whitaker entered that London pub during the Christmas period of 1943, he too was bored. He was fed up with the waiting. Preparations for Operation Overlord were in full flow. They were training for it, but there was no indication of when it would take place.

Even for Whitaker, a celebrated hero of the war, this gloomy winter was taking its toll. The cold, wet, relentless training in the Hampshire countryside had become too much.

Therefore, the chance encounter with the officer from the USO in that pub invigorated him. He had little pushback from the Canadians' Chief of Staff when he approached him with the idea at the Canadian Military Headquarters.

Lieutenant-General Kenneth Stuart and Whitaker had a history from their time together at the RMC. The Tea Bowl had been given a date: February 13, 1944, at White City Stadium in west London. The game was on.

As we have discovered, the Canadians were blessed with talent, 'It really was an all-star East-West team when we finally put it together,' said Denis Whitaker. 'There was quite a few Toronto Argonauts stationed in Britain, including Captain George Hees, Captain Ken Turnbull, as well as Don Grant, a half-back, Bill Drinkwater, and Fred Brown. We were lucky to get Hulk Welsh, one of Canada's greatest punters, who played for the Hamilton Tigers and Montreal Wing Wheelers.'

The two-time Grey Cup winner and three-time Western All-Star, Jeff Nicklin, was brought in as the Canadians' back.

Fullback Andy Bieber was a team-mate of Nicklin's at the Blue Bombers and he won the Grey Cup with them in 1939 and 1941. Alongside these Winnipeg winners was another Grey Cup champion, Orville Burke.

Added to the all-star cast of CFL icons in Europe was Sarnia's All-Star centre, Nick Paithouski.

Whitaker was constructing a roster fit for a Grey Cup. Paul 'Pappy' Rowe of the Calgary Bronks was another All-Star back.

There were around 30 players signed up for the Canadian Mustangs. Their coach was Major Chicks Mundell, a doctor in the Army Medical Corps. Mundell had played football at Queen's and coached Denis Whitaker at RMC. Their training was hard, but it was a welcome break from the rigours of the war.

If the Americans were anticipating an easy game, they were about to be in for a big shock. There is no doubt they would not have expected to be facing the Canadian Football League's All-Pro line-up.

It was decided that the game would be played half under American rules with American referees, and half under Canadian rules with Canadian referees.

There have been many rule changes to Canadian football since the mid-1940s. The American game has remained true to its original form, apart from a few adjustments. Even in the 1940s, both the American and Canadian formats were different, which was a test for both teams.

Denis Whitaker said, 'We had, in fact, to learn two completely separate sets of plays and strategies for the two halves. Paul Rowe, who once played for Oregon, was a great help in developing our American offence.'

Whitaker and his team were taking this contest seriously. Victory for the Canadians would provide a massive shot in the arm after a dreary winter.

* * *

The game had captured the imagination of the Americans. A preview article appeared in the *Stars and Stripes* publication on February 4, 1944. The reporter, Gene Graff, wrote, 'Football smacking of international flavour will be the dish Sunday, Feb. 13, when the CBS Pirates tackle the Canadian Army Mustangs in the "Tea Bowl" game at White City Stadium before an anticipated throng of 25,000 Allied forces and civilian fans.'

Graff also wrote, 'The contest, marking the first time American and Canadian gridders have squared off since the war began, will be an interesting experiment in comparative merits of football as played in the neighbouring countries. Determined by the flip of a coin, American rules will be observed in the first half, while the second will be played according to Canadian style.'

At that time the main variations between the two countries were: the Canadians scored five points for a touchdown instead of the six in the American League; Canadian rules had three downs to advance ten yards; and blocking beyond the line of scrimmage was prohibited by the Canucks.

Canada had no restriction on the number of players in the backfield who were allowed to be in motion before the ball was snapped. And there was the rouge, the CFL's quirky rule where the kicking team is awarded a point if the team either misses a field goal or punts the football, and the receiving team does not get the ball out of their end zone.

The game was billed as having colourful pageantry, including marching bands, organised cheering sections and half-time entertainment. It was bringing the best of football, and a taste of home, for troops from both North American countries.

News of the game was filtering across Canada. *Canadian Press* had sent a preview piece on its wires; even the small town of Lethbridge in Alberta, which is 132 miles south of Calgary, was running it in the Tuesday sports section of the *Lethbridge Herald* on February 1. Its headline read, 'Canucks to Battle Yanks in "Tea Bowl."'

The article listed Canada's stellar line-up and details of the event. Whitaker's beer-fuelled brainwave was making international headlines.

CHAPTER 16

The Tea Bowl, February 13, 1944

'I loved the game and besides, we got out of the army for two months'

– Ken Turnbull, end, Canadian Mustangs

AFTER WEEKS of training, game day had finally arrived. Denis Whitaker's Canadian Mustangs had assembled, and they were ready to go. 'February 13, we arrived at White City Stadium feeling pretty optimistic about our chances,' recalled Whitaker. 'I guess we were in a minority in that respect because the odds were 15/1 for the Americans.'

The assembly of the American Army Pirates had been overseen by their captain, Private First Class Frank Dombrowski.

A who's who of military hierarchy was in attendance, with top-ranking officials from both armies in the stands. A London silversmith had also been commissioned to produce an eight-inch silver teapot as the trophy.

The BBC provided the broadcast transmission for the American Forces Network. The transmitter was set up for 2.35pm and the broadcast continued throughout the afternoon, with an agreement to cover the entirety of the game and no cut to the studio at half-time. Private First Class Jameson provided play-by-play for the first half of the game. Captain Ted Leather was the announcer for the second half, when the Canadian rules were played. Corporal John Vrotsos took over commentary of the half-time festivities.

The operations room gave instructions to cut to the *Andre Kostelanetz* programme if the game had finished by 4.40pm 'If any later, merely fill with Kostelanetz records and from five o'clock onwards carry on with regular schedule.'

This game had given so many young men something to focus on, and a goal to work towards. The Canadians were ready, they believed in the talent they possessed and had formed a comradeship over the previous six weeks of practice. Just looking around the locker room they could see MVPs, All-Stars, league scoring leaders.

'The *esprit de corps* was terrific,' said Ken Turnbull. 'Our team were damned good fellows, and we were serious about winning.'

Spitfires circled over the stadium, on the lookout for the German Luftwaffe, although Turnbull had no recollection of them. 'I wasn't really paying attention to any action up there,' he recalled. 'It makes sense, though. There was an awful lot of talent in one small place – 30,000 combat troops and two Canadian generals.'

Puzzled British spectators were provided with explainers inside the gameday programme. The atmosphere within the stadium was electric, with massed Canadian pipe bands and the US European Theater of Operations Band performing classic hits such as 'In the Mood' and 'Chattanooga Choo-Choo'. This sporting event had become a celebration of the Allies. Revenue generated from the game was for the benefit of the British Red Cross and St John fund.

If there was pressure on the Canadian Mustangs with such high-profile names in the crowd, they did not feel it. The first half was tight and left little to the imagination as it ended scoreless. The Americans failed to capitalise on their own rules, while their opponents from the north held firm.

In Canadian football, an emphasis is put on the kicking game, which is why the rouge works so effectively. The long punts from the Canadian Mustangs kept pinning the US Pirates back. Lieutenant Andy Bieber's long, towering punts repulsed the Americans whenever they neared the Canadians' territory.

The Pirates tried attacking through the air in the second quarter with halfbacks Corporal Ben Detterman and Private First-Class Basil Russ alternating pitches. The Mustangs' defence went toe-to-toe with the American receivers and kept them at bay. There were nine pass attempts by the Pirates in the first half, and only a 14-yard gain from Detterman to Sergeant Frank Bartoni, a 185-pound end from New York, was completed.

After the interval, the Canadian all-stars attacked with guile on offence. They outran the Americans and dominated through the air. Where the Yanks had struggled to move the ball with their own rules in the first two quarters, the Canucks were taking advantage in the second half.

The US Pirates received the kick-off to start the third quarter. Their attempts at running the ball were thwarted by the Canadian defence. Playing to the CFL three-down rule, the Americans punted. Major Denis Whitaker received the kick and ran at will to the Pirates' 36-yard line.

The movement and passing from the Mustangs had the Pirates flummoxed. They were not accustomed to the wide-open lateral passing game of the Canadians. 'We opened the scoring five minutes into the third quarter,' explained Whitaker.

Denis Whitaker's wide lateral to Lieutenant Orville Burke took the Mustangs to the American 18-yard line. Two plays later they found the end zone in unconventional fashion. Whitaker fumbled Burke's pass as he advanced eight yards to the Pirates' 10-yard line. Canadian rules allow a player to kick the loose ball, which is what Ken Turnbull did. He spotted the free ball and booted it across the goal line, where he pounced on the ball for the touchdown. Whitaker kicked the extra point.

'I think the Americans had more problems adjusting to our game than we did to theirs,' remembered Turnbull years later. 'I'm a little embarrassed to admit it now, but I got a touchdown in a funny way. The ball was loose, I kicked it over the goal line. The Americans forgot that we were playing different rules.'

Basil Russ was instrumental for the Americans on their resulting drive. A holding call on Russ's incomplete pass put the ball on the Pirates' 40. Russ threw the ball again on the next play. Detterman was the target; he grabbed the ball and took it to their 48.

Russ and Detterman were clicking. The next play was another pass from Russ; it was long and found Detterman at the Canadian 30-yard line. Detterman evaded Mustang defenders and found the end zone. Russ connected with Corporal John Venezia, a 140-pound halfback from Detroit, for the conversion and tied the score at 6-6.

Young Ben Russ had felt too anxious to play in this game but found himself excelling on the biggest stage of his football career. He and Detterman were the bright sparks for the US Pirates.

For the Canadians, Whitaker and Orville Burke were outstanding. The game was finely poised for the large crowd as it entered the final quarter. It had just begun when Burke threw a 20-yard pass to Whitaker, who took it home for the touchdown.

Any momentum that the Americans had gathered in their scoring play before the fourth quarter was lost. They continued to struggle with the Canadian rules as they anxiously tried to move the ball forward.

Canadian supporters were on their feet, especially those clinching on to their betting receipts, knowing a huge payday was about to come their way. With 20 seconds remaining, the Mustangs iced the game for Canada. Orville Burke intercepted a pass from the Americans deep into Pirates territory. Burke outsmarted his opponents on the next play, lining up without a huddle and taking the snap while the Americans were caught napping.

Jeff Nicklin, who had been granted last-minute leave from his parachute battalion, speared the ball at the one-yard line and stepped over the goal line at the final whistle. The Canadians triumphed 16-6.

'The stands went crazy,' said Denis Whitaker. 'Particularly the Canadian soldiers who had won more money in a day than many of them had earned in a year. In fact, days later Canadian soldiers could still be seen wandering through London in battledress yelling, "We're number one."'

The Americans received much better pay than the Canadians. A Canadian private's pay was only 30 cents a day and captains were given $6. The betting was heavy and the Americans were willing to give the odds, which the Canucks took full advantage of.

'After the game I had a date with a lovely lady from the Red Cross,' recalled Ken Turnbull. 'It was a first date, and I took her to the Grosvenor House Hotel for dinner where the food was fantastic, and we ordered a terrific meal. Just as they brought the soup course the air raid siren sounded, and we had to leave. When the raid was over, we tried to get back, but they would not serve us.'

On Valentine's Day, Captain Ted Leather broadcast this sportscast for CBC (Canadian Broadcasting Corporation):

Good evening, Canada.

Yesterday afternoon thousands of Canadian and American soldiers and their somewhat puzzled English friends packed the stands at White City Stadium to see an All-Star Canadian grid squad win the first Tea Bowl classic rugby game from the American Army Pirates by 16-6. The first half was played under American eastern collegiate rules and while the Canadian lads couldn't seem to get their end runs away around the unaccustomed interference, they held the Yanks to no score at half-time.

From the start of the second frame the Maple Leaf squad took things into their own hands with the Pirates sticking to their own brand of game and being consistently outmanoeuvred by Army's open up passing tactics and the long high punts of Andy Bieber and Huck Welch. Opening score came in the first few minutes of the period when Major Denny Whitaker of the Hamilton Tigers threw a long pass to Orville Burke of Rough Riders fame which was intercepted, fumbled, and finally kicked across the Americans' goal line where Captain Ken Turnbull, Toronto Balmy Beach, fell neatly on the loose ball for the opening counter. Whitaker, who also captained and coached the team, placed the convert neatly between the uprights for the conversion.

After another five minutes of hard pressing tactics, Basil Russ for the Yankees intercepted a loose pass and ran the ball back for an American first down on the centre field mark. On two quick plays, both forward passes from Russ to Detterman, the Americans marched up the field for their first

> and only touchdown of the game, tying things up when Detterman took the convert.
>
> With the fourth quarter opening scores tied, the fans really went wild in the good old Canadian style. Welch's long high kicks consistently kept the American boys back in their own territory and when George Hees fell on a long loose ball, Orville Burke, who played one of the greatest games of his career, threw a 40-yard pass to Denny Whitaker, who romped home in the clear for the second Canadian counter. The convert going wild, the score set at 11-6 until one minute to go.
>
> With Canadians in the clear on their opponents' 10-yard line, Burke threw another cross-field pass that found husky Jeff Nicklin, the Blue Bombers' stellar end man in position to cross the line just as the closing whistle rolled out the game for a 16-6 victory.
>
> The game was played complete with attendance of the hierarchy of both Armies, the massed pipe bands of two Canadian divisions, and the headquarter band of the US Central Base Section.
>
> Major John Donovan of Harvard and Boston gridirons paid a visit to the Canuck dressing rooms after the game and told the boys just what he and his team thought about the whole thing, being greeted with three rousing Tiger cheers which he was asked to take back to his G.I.s with the boys' compliments. All in all, the Tea Bowl game will go down as one of the biggest and best international goodwill gestures of Canada's and America's sporting histories.

Denis Whitaker cherished the silver teapot, and it remained in his possession until the day he died. Speaking with

Shelagh Whitaker in 1996, Denny said, 'I imagine a lot of those soldiers who saw the game kept memories too, that might have helped keep them sane in the months to come.'

Operation Overlord was looming large on the horizon. Many men were about to have their worlds turned upside down.

Whitaker had only intended on the Tea Bowl being a one-off game. The Americans, however, do not like losing and they had other ideas.

A rematch was percolating, and it was too good for those in Canada's hierarchy to resist.

CHAPTER 17

The Coffee Bowl, March 19, 1944

'In the second game, they definitely had some imports. One guy who had been captain of the Chicago Bears in November in the States was playing against us in England in March'

– Ken Turnbull, end, Canadian Mustangs

AFTER SUFFERING such a heavy and embarrassing loss in front of a huge crowd, the Americans wanted a chance to redeem themselves. The Canadian rules had caught them off guard. There is no doubt that they were also surprised to confront such an all-star roster.

Lieutenant-General Ken Stuart, the chief of staff at the Canadian Military Headquarters, was equally keen on another game. Stuart was so eager, he demanded that the Canadians fielded their best team, regardless of duties required by the troops elsewhere. They had been granted six weeks' leave for what had initially been intended to be a one-off shootout game. On March 3, 1944, Stuart sent a memorandum requesting some of Canada's stars to be released:

> I am most anxious that the Canadian Army should field as strong a team as possible for our return match with the US Army.

I understand this game will take place on 19 March '44. We are having considerable difficulty in fielding as strong a team as we would like. Will you please find out for me whether the following officers can be available? They are urgently required to strengthen the side.

Major J. A. Nicklin, 1 Para Bn – Bulford

Major G. E. Armstrong – Uckfield 427

Lieut. Grayson, S. Sask. R. – Worthing 4554

This officer reported to the coach but has recently been called back to his unit. I would like to know why he was called back.

Will you please put somebody on to this and let me know results earliest?

* * *

Remember, Jeff Nicklin was a tough disciplinarian. He demanded full commitment in preparation, both from himself and his battalion. Nicklin was a last-minute call-up to the Mustangs roster for the Tea Bowl game weeks earlier. But he wanted to be back with his battalion and continue training for the forthcoming invasion of Normandy. He did not want to risk himself with injury. Ironically, he jumped with his parachute on the eve of D-Day deep into enemy territory with a shoulder injury that he sustained when playing a football game for his troops just days before the invasion.

Tension was building among the Canadian hierarchy and on March 7, Major-General P.J. Montague sent a memo to Nicklin's commanding officer at the 1st Canadian Parachute Battalion. It read:

Major J.A. Nicklin

1. The Chief of Staff is aware that the m/n will not be playing in the return football match with the

> US Army, and I am directed to inform you that he is in agreement with the reasons given for Major Nicklin's non-participation.

By this time the rematch had been given an official title, the Coffee Bowl, and the PR was in full flow.

The *Canadian Press* reported, 'London's huge White City Stadium never saw such a game as that first encounter when the Canadian Mustangs defeated the American Pirates 16-6 before a crowd of 30,000 Canadians, Americans, and Britons. The return contest is expected to draw 40,000.'

There was no surprise when the Americans announced that they were to field a new team called the Blue Division. The Coffee Bowl would flip the halves, so it was Canadian rules to start and American rules after the interval. A silver coffee pot was also commissioned for the victors.

Among the replacements for the Canadian team was Hank Living, the former centre for the Toronto Argonauts. Joining him as one of the newcomers on the roster was his Argos team-mate Bill Stukus, whose brother, Annis Stukus, was also a former Toronto Argonaut. Annis Stukus would become coach of the new Edmonton franchise and often took on their kicking duties, even as their general manager. He also oversaw the BC Lions as they were introduced to the league as an expansion club. Annis Stukus was enshrined in the Canadian Football Hall of Fame. The Annis Stukus Trophy is presented each year to the CFL's Coach of the Year.

Incidentally, Bill and Annis were not the only siblings graced with football ability. Their brother Frank was a member of the 1938 Grey Cup-winning Toronto Argonauts team alongside them.

American officials were not just rolling out anyone who could play football with their Blue Division line-up. The

Infantry Division Blues were the GI champions of the ETO (European Theater of Operations).

The high-flying Blues were coached by Second Lieutenant James Holston and had remained unbeaten in his four games in charge. Holston was noted as having his players prepared for the Canadian rules in this match-up. That was no doubt an order that had been demanded from higher ranking officials, and there would be no napping during those expansive plays and no-huddle offences. The Americans had been fooled once; they were not going to let that happen again.

One of the immediate changes the Americans made was to their defensive line. They wanted to create a formidable obstacle for Canadian runners. The Americans had the Chicago Bears centre, Steward Clarkson and Lieutenant Forest Ferguson, an All-American end who had dominated with the US Army All-Stars.

Leading up to the game, the Blues were made to sweat over the availability of Sergeant Tommy Thompson, the versatile quarterback from the Philadelphia Eagles. Military duties had kept Thompson out of the Blues' previous two games.

The Americans' plan was to fill their backfield with power when the Canadian rules were in play, providing speed and strength when motion was granted before the snap of the ball. Corporal Johnny Bayne was a player that the Canucks had to be wary of as the contest approached, with his ability to run and catch.

There were initial fears that Denis Whitaker would be missing for the rematch. Since the first game, Whitaker had been promoted from major and the concerns were that his duties would forbid him from taking part. However, he did manage to make the team for the Coffee Bowl. George Hees joined Jeff Nicklin as another key absentee from the original victorious Mustangs roster.

* * *

Game day arrived on March 19, 1944. A crowd of 50,000 spectators packed into White City Stadium for the highly anticipated rematch. Some reports had mentioned 55,000 were in attendance. The BBC again provided the feed for the American Forces Network, with Private First Class Keith Jameson and Corporal John Vrotsos calling the play-by-play commentary. Tickets for this contest were free of charge.

Desperate to punish the Mustangs with their own rules, the Americans came charging out of the traps at the start of the game. They took command almost immediately, with the Philadelphia Eagles' Tommy Thompson putting in an MVP performance.

Thompson had the Canucks on their heels, consistently picking up yardage from scrimmage. He was returning kicks, running the ball, and effortlessly driving the Blues into Mustangs territory with his clinical passing. The Canadian rules were not fazing this NFL star.

Canada received the kick-off and the Mustangs' wingback, Sergeant Floyd Brown, fluffed his lines. He fumbled the return, and it was swooped upon by the Blues' right tackle, Private First Class Joe Long. Long had put his team in excellent field position at the Canadian 35-yard line.

Tommy Thompson and the Blues took the ball to the six-yard line on the resulting drive. However, the series was thwarted when Orville Burke intercepted Thompson's pass.

The Mustangs struggled to gain any momentum and soon the Americans were back deep into Canadian territory. Once again, Thompson was intercepted. This time it was Denis Whitaker with the pick, snatching the ball from Thompson's intended pass for Forest Ferguson at the 15-yard line.

A score was coming, and it was the Americans who got it. A poor kick by the Mustangs' Sergeant Joe Bell set the Blues up. Johnny Bayne returned the ball to the Canadians' 18-yard line. Thompson took the snap, stepped back, examined the field, and launched a pass to Bayne in the end zone. The resulting kick was blocked, and the Americans went in at half-time with a 5-0 lead.

Just as they had done five weeks earlier throughout the duration of the Tea Bowl, Spitfires circled over the area in case the Germans tried to sneak a raid. There were even more service personnel and military hierarchy gathered in the same place for this event than last time.

Into the second half and NFL rules applied. Stewart 'Tex' Clarkson, the former Chicago Bears star, was dominant in the blocking game. The Mustangs went for it on fourth and one midway through the third quarter, but Orville Burke was smothered by the Americans' defensive line on the 29-yard line. That set the Blues up with excellent field position to start their drive.

Thompson opened the series with a run to the 17. Six minutes into the third quarter, the Eagles star found Johnny Bayne again. The ball sailed through the arms of the Blues' Sergeant Dave Swanson and bounced off his chest into the hands of the elusive Bayne, who was conveniently behind the goal line. The conversion, this time, was made. 12-0 USA.

Bayne got his hat-trick early in the final quarter. Tommy Thompson returned Huck Welch's long punt from the Blues' 18-yard line to the 30. A combination of Thompson's running and Bayne's ball carrying ploughed the Americans to the Mustangs' 10. Johnny Bayne ran up the left on a reverse from Thompson and scored. The conversion was missed, but the Americans had an 18-0 lead with time running out for the Canucks.

In the final minutes, the desperate Canadians trudged upfield. Quarterback Orville Burke completed 30-yard passes to Winnipeg's Andy Bieber and Toronto collegiate star, Sergeant Red Bell. Denis Whitaker was not shying away from his defensive responsibilities, regularly hitting Tommy Thompson with hard tackles when it looked as though the American had room for big gains.

It was all in vain for the Canadian Mustangs, and the mighty Infantry Division Blues, the ETO champions, remained undefeated.

The 'coincidental' appearance in England of several American pros did not go unnoticed by the Canucks. 'In the second game, they definitely had some imports,' recalled Ken Turnbull. 'One guy who had been captain of the Chicago Bears in November in the States was playing against us in England in March.'

Another Canadian told Denis Whitaker decades later, 'I came face to face with this guy with a deep suntan. Remember, we're in England and it was March. They'd brought this guy in from Hawaii. So, we lost. But the first game? We beat those sons-of-bitches.'

* * *

A few days after the Coffee Bowl had been played, a feature was written for the *Canadian Press* about the British perspective of gridiron football. Allan Nickelson wrote the report, and it featured in Canadian papers such as the *Medicine Hat Daily News* on March 21.

The headline was 'British Baffled: Sure Canadian-American Style of Football Will Never Supplant Soccer in Old Country'.

Nickelson had spoken to Len and Peter at a crowded London pub. He referred to them as 'typical English soccer fans' and according to his conversation, they believed that gridiron football would never be a threat to the beautiful game of football that they admired.

Len and Peter had both attended the Tea Bowl game on February 13. It was their first experience of gridiron action and, although they enjoyed it, they believed football, their football, was far superior. The continuous flow of football that's long been associated with the English game was far better, in their opinion, than the stop-start nature of American/Canadian football.

'We found it got a little boring watching the players go into the huddle,' they told Nickelson. 'They clasped their arms around each other, their heads together as though they were discussing the second front. Then, too, we got a little tired at times of watching players on one another. But we jumped to our feet with the rest when a back threw a long forward pass or when the backs combined on a sweeping run around the ends and tossed the ball around to each other.'

Len and Peter admitted that the rules were overwhelming at times and were increasingly complicated when the game changed from the American regulations to Canadian. That first game would have been a dull affair for novice supporters, especially the first half. Even the most dedicated fans want to see touchdowns scored. The Canadians had a strict defensive plan during the period of game under American rules.

One of Len and Peter was a factory worker, the other was a bricklayer. They and the reported 5,000 Britons at White City Stadium for the Tea Bowl game were left wanting more. Meanwhile, unsurprisingly, the 17,000 Canadians that were present had said it was as good as a heavyweight fixture back in Canada.

The expansive play that came with the CFL rules appealed more to the first-time watchers. They enjoyed how it allowed players to be open more, despite the extra man on the field.

Allan Nickelson had also commented on how the public transport was affected by the huge crowd. He wrote, 'Some of the toughest work of the Sunday afternoon fixture, played in the mammoth White City Stadium, was done by members of the crowd. Tubes, buses, and trolleys were crammed. At many Tube stations the crowds were so great that hundreds did not arrive until half-time.'

A correspondent for the former British tabloid, the *Daily Sketch,* wrote, 'A new link was cemented between the two nations – well, that's about all I can say. Exactly what happened in this game is nobody's business.'

In reference to the players, the writer noted, 'They were padded all over and wore crash helmets,' and added, 'I don't blame them.'

Perhaps that writer, as well as Len and Peter, witnessed the day the NFL brought pre-season games to London in the 1980s. The fact that 36 regular season games have been played in the UK over a 16-year period will have blown their minds. Any talk of London ever having a team, a European league involving German teams, and the Americans playing multiple regular season games in Germany would have been ridiculed as nonsense.

Len and Peter were right. Eighty years later, football as they knew it still reigns supreme in England.

The Tea and Coffee Bowls were the perfect oasis for the young football stars who were caught up in a seemingly never-ending war. Some of them had brothers killed in action, fathers who had died back home and they could not be there to say goodbye. There were twenty-somethings like 28-year-old Denis Whitaker (he turned 29 before the rematch) who had seen fellow soldiers killed around him in bloody battles such as Dieppe. Suddenly he found himself responsible for making the decisions that could cost the lives of men who were a similar age, others still boys. He had also become a paternal figure to them despite only being young himself. The horrors these sports-stars-turned-soldiers had experienced is unimaginable. So, to play football for three hours in front of a packed crowd must have brought great joy to their lives. Even if it was brief, the relief they felt would have been like winning the lottery. Some may have even smiled for the first time since they could remember.

CHAPTER 18

Players Lost

'There were stellar performances on the field by some of these players and more importantly, there were stellar performances on the battlefield'

– Joe Horrigan, former executive director of the Pro Football Hall of Fame

WITH WAR comes tragedy. Millions of families around the world had their lives torn apart by the loss of loved ones who bravely served their countries during the Second World War. So many lives were taken from young men just a generation after the First World War had taken a death toll that had been unfathomable.

There were more than 900 men from the NFL, players and personnel, who served in World War II. The conflicts claimed the lives of 23 men who related to the league. Twenty-one of them were active or former players. The others were a former head coach and a team executive.

The Pro Football Hall of Fame has honoured the men:

Lt. **Chuck Braidwood** (E, Portsmouth-Cleveland-Cardinals-Cincinnati, 1930–1933) – Member of Red Cross. Killed in South Pacific, winter 1944–1945

Cpl. **Mike Basca** (HB, Philadelphia, 1941) – Killed in France in 1944

Lt. **Charlie Behan** (E, Detroit, 1942) – Killed on Okinawa in 1945

Maj. **Keith Birlem** (E, Cardinals-Washington, 1939) – Killed trying to land combat damaged bomber in England in 1943

Lt. **Al Blozis** (T, Giants, 1942–44) – Killed in France, 1945

Lt. **Young Bussey** (QB, Bears, 1940–41) – Killed in Philippines landing assault in 1944

Lt. **Jack Chevigny** (Coach, Cardinals, 1932) – Killed on Iwo Jima in 1945

Capt. **Ed Doyle** (E, Frankford-Pottsville, 1924–25) – Killed during North Africa invasion in 1942

Lt. Col. **Grassy Hinton** (B, Staten Island, 1932) – Killed in plane crash in East Indies in 1944

Capt. **Smiley Johnson** (G, Green Bay, 1940–41) – Killed on Iwo Jima in 1945

Lt. **Eddie Kahn** (G, Boston/Washington, 1935–37) – Died from wounds suffered during Leyte invasion in 1945

Sgt. **Alex Ketzko** (T, Detroit, 1943) – Killed in France in 1944

Capt. **Lee Kizzire** (FB, Detroit, 1937) – Shot down near New Guinea in 1943

Lt. **Jack Lummus** (E, Giants, 1941) – Killed on Iwo Jima in 1945

Bob Mackert (T, Rochester Jeffersons, 1925)

Frank Maher (B, Pittsburgh-Cleveland Rams, 1941)

Pvt. **Jim Mooney** (E-G-FB, Newark-Brooklyn-Cincinnati-St Louis-Cardinals, 1930–37) – Killed by sniper in France in 1944

Lt. **John O'Keefe** (Front office, Philadelphia) – Killed flying a patrol mission in Panama Canal Zone

Chief Spec. **Gus Sonnenberg** (B, Buffalo-Columbus-Detroit-Providence, 1923–28, 1930) – Died of illness at Bethesda Naval Hospital in 1944

Lt. **Len Supulski** (E, Philadelphia, 1942) – Killed in plane crash in Nebraska in 1944
Lt. **Don Wemple** (E, Brooklyn, 1941) – Killed in plane crash in India in 1944
Lt. **Chet Wetterlund** (HB, Cardinals-Detroit, 1942) – Killed in plane crash off New Jersey coast in 1944
Capt. **Waddy Young** (E, Brooklyn, 1939–40) – Killed in plane crash following first B-29 raid on Tokyo in 1945

* * *

The former New York Giants end, Jack Lummus, was awarded a posthumous Congressional Medal of Honor, which is the country's highest military honour. Lummus was a Marine fighting in Japan.

His Medal of Honor citation at the National World War II Museum in New Orleans reads:

> For conspicuous gallantry and intrepidity at the risk of his life above and beyond the call of duty as leader of a Rifle Platoon attached to the 2d Battalion, 27th Marines, 5th Marine Division, in action against enemy Japanese forces on Iwo Jima in the Volcano Islands, 8 March 1945. Resuming his assault tactics with bold decision after fighting without respite for 2 days and nights, 1st Lt. Lummus slowly advanced his platoon against an enemy deeply entrenched in a network of mutually supporting positions. Suddenly halted by a terrific concentration of hostile fire, he unhesitatingly moved forward of his front lines in an effort to neutralize the Japanese position. Although knocked to the ground when an enemy grenade exploded close by, he immediately recovered himself and, again moving forward despite the intensified barrage, quickly located, attacked, and destroyed the

occupied emplacement. Instantly taken under fire by the garrison of a supporting pillbox and further assailed by the slashing fury of hostile rifle fire, he fell under the impact of a second enemy grenade but, courageously disregarding painful shoulder wounds, staunchly continued his heroic 1-man assault and charged the second pillbox, annihilating all the occupants. Subsequently returning to his platoon position, he fearlessly traversed his lines under fire, encouraging his men to advance and directing the fire of supporting tanks against other stubbornly holding Japanese emplacements.

Held up again by a devastating barrage, he again moved into the open, rushed a third heavily fortified installation and killed the defending troops. Determined to crush all resistance, he led his men indomitably, personally attacking foxholes and spider traps with his carbine and systematically reducing the fanatic opposition until, stepping on a land mine, he sustained fatal wounds. By his outstanding valor, skilled tactics, and tenacious perseverance in the face of overwhelming odds, 1st Lt. Lummus had inspired his stout-hearted Marines to continue the relentless drive northward, thereby contributing materially to the success of his regimental mission. His dauntless leadership and unwavering devotion to duty throughout sustain and enhance the highest traditions of the US Naval Service. He gallantly gave his life in the service of his country.

Maurice Britt played for the Detroit Lions in 1941 before being called up for service. He survived the war. Along with Lummus, Britt was one of three men connected to the NFL who received their country's highest honour for their service in the Second World War.

Maurice Britt's Congressional Medal of Honor citation is:

> For conspicuous gallantry and intrepidity at the risk of his life above and beyond the call of duty. Disdaining enemy hand grenades and close-range machine pistols, machine guns, and rifles, Lt. Britt inspired and led a handful of his men in repelling a bitter counterattack by approximately 100 Germans against his company positions north of Mignano, Italy, on the morning of 10 November 1943.
>
> During the intense firefight, Lt. Britt's canteen and field glasses were shattered; a bullet pierced his side; his chest, face, and hands were covered with grenade wounds. Despite his wounds, for which he refused to accept medical attention until ordered to do so by his battalion commander following the battle, he personally killed five and wounded an unknown number of Germans, wiped out one enemy machine-gun crew, fired five clips of carbine and an undetermined amount of M-1 rifle ammunition, and threw 32 fragmentation grenades.
>
> His bold, aggressive actions, utterly disregarding superior enemy numbers, resulted in capture of four Germans, two of them wounded, and enabled several captured Americans to escape. Lt. Britt's undaunted courage and prowess in arms were largely responsible for repulsing a German counterattack which, if successful, would have isolated his battalion and destroyed his company.

Joe Foss was the third Congressional Medal of Honor recipient. Like Britt, he survived the war. Foss became a television broadcaster and the commissioner of the American Football League, which rivalled the National Football League before the merger in 1966.

Foss's citation reads:

> For outstanding heroism and courage above and beyond the call of duty as Executive Officer of a Marine Fighting Squadron, at Guadalcanal, Solomon Islands. Engaging in almost daily combat with the enemy from October 9 to November 19, 1942, Captain Foss personally shot down 23 Japanese aircraft and damaged others so severely that their destruction was extremely probable.
>
> In addition, during this period, he successfully led a large number of escort missions, skilfully covering reconnaissance, bombing and photographic planes as well as surface craft.
>
> On January 15, 1943, he added three more enemy aircraft to his already brilliant successes for a record of aerial combat achievement unsurpassed in this war. Boldly searching out an approaching enemy force on January 25, Captain Foss led his eight F4F Marine planes and four Army P-38s into action and, undaunted by tremendously superior numbers, intercepted and struck with such force that four Japanese fighters were shot down and the bombers were turned back without releasing a single bomb. His remarkable flying skill, inspiring leadership and indomitable fighting spirit were distinctive factors in the defense of strategic American positions on Guadalcanal.

It is difficult, nigh on impossible, to understand what it was like for these young men to put down their equipment, pause their careers, wave goodbye to wives, children, mothers, fathers, brothers, and sisters to fight for their country. Many of them did it because they felt it was what they needed to do. Some paid the ultimate price: newlyweds like Canadian football stars Charles 'Hank' Living and Jeff Nicklin. Nicklin's son never had the chance to meet his father.

Denis Whitaker, whose wife had given birth to his daughter while he was thousands of miles away, was unsure of when he would meet his first born. What would he have been feeling that tragic day at Dieppe as thousands were dying all around him?

These men are a tiny fraction of the millions who sacrificed everything. So many, tragically, never returned home.

Their bravery was not in vain, and they will be remembered, always.

On the eve of the CFL's Western Final in 2023, the Winnipeg Blue Bombers' head coach Mike O'Shea voiced his frustration at the league's decision to move the division finals from Sunday to Saturday. It meant the games were played on Remembrance Day, November 11. 'To be perfectly honest, if I had my say we probably wouldn't be playing on Remembrance Day. But I don't make the schedule,' O'Shea said.

The coach has strong connections to the military. His father served in the British Royal Air Force during the Second World War and his grandfather fought for the British infantry in the First World War. O'Shea has taken a keen interest in Winnipeg's military background, and for the pre-game press conference he was wearing his poppy along with an RCAF (Royal Canadian Air Force) hat he picked up at the store on the local base.

CHAPTER 19

Wartime Rivalry

'You only get out of life what you put into it'

– Chicago Bears Hall of Fame quarterback, Sid Luckman

WHILE THE war raged around the world, football reluctantly continued in the United States. Though hundreds of the NFL's players had been posted overseas, some star talent remained.

The Chicago Bears and Washington Redskins were the two powerhouses in the NFL throughout the early 1940s. On December 26, 1943, they found themselves facing off again in another Championship Game.

Their owners, George Halas of the Bears and George Preston Marshall of the Redskins, were the visionaries of the sport. The duo had been partly responsible for some of the rule changes that had been introduced ten years earlier, in 1933.

They had collaborated among some of the other owners in adopting new regulations that helped speed up the game and made it a more entertaining product. For example, they moved the hashmarks closer to the centre of the field, so there was more room for the players to operate between the markings and the sidelines. This made runs and passes easier to manoeuvre around the field. These seem glaringly obvious now, but without their innovation the product that has become a worldwide billion-dollar business might not exist.

By no means was the game of that era the pass-heavy spectacle that it is now. They changed it so the passer – quarterback was not an official title at that time – no longer had to be more than five yards behind the line of scrimmage when throwing the ball. The pass could be made from anywhere, so long as it was behind the line.

In '33 it was voted that the goal posts be moved to the back of the end zone. This was to reduce the number of tied games with increased field goal opportunities. Mike Richman, the author of *The Redskins Encyclopaedia*, explained, 'It was all with a goal of making it more of an entertaining product and bringing more fans to the stadiums. That was actually one of George Preston Marshall's claims to fame. He was very entertainment conscious. And he even wanted more women to come out and watch the games too.'

One of the great sights at modern games is families of all ages and genders celebrating the fast, ferocious sport of American football. Huge crowds come together and cheer exceptional athletic performances while singing along to music, or marvel at cheerleaders and firework displays. More than 80 years after his vision for sport entertainment, Preston Marshall's brainwave has generated billions for the league and its owners, while producing the biggest single sporting event in the world with the Super Bowl.

Two of the best quarterbacks of that 1930s–1940s era, Sid Luckman and Sammy Baugh, squared off for the third time in four years at pro football's biggest game, the NFL Championship Game. They were 1-1 against one another heading into the 1943 showpiece.

The Bears quarterback, Sid Luckman, was drafted by the team second overall in 1939. The following year he had led them to the title game, and that record 73-0 win over Sammy Baugh's Redskins. However, Luckman only completed four of six passes for 102 yards in that drubbing. On the second play from scrimmage, fullback Bill Osmanski – sprung by a George Wilson block that wiped out two Washington defenders – dashed 68 yards for a touchdown.

Emotions were high before that 1940 Championship Game because the Redskins had beaten Chicago 7-3 in Washington a few weeks earlier. Larry Mayer, a senior writer for the Chicago Bears, wrote about that famous match-up as part of a lookback feature for the team's website. He reported about an issue after the game when the Bears complained that Washington should have been penalised for pass interference in the end zone on the final play. George Preston Marshall then called the Bears cry-babies, quitters, and frontrunners.

So, leading up to the showpiece, Halas showed his players newspaper clippings of Marshall's comments and told them in the locker room before the game: 'Gentlemen, this is what George Preston Marshall thinks of you. Well, I think you're a great football team, the greatest ever assembled. Now, go out there on the field and prove it!' And that's exactly what they did. No team has ever scored more points than the 73 they did on that day. The Miami Dolphins came close in Week 3 of the 2023 season, when they beat the Denver Broncos 70-20.

Washington and Baugh had their revenge in 1942, though Chicago had the better season in '43. The Bears, in the absence of head coach George Halas, ended the 1943 regular season 8-1-1 and had lost to the Redskins 21-7 in Week 10. In that game, Luckman had completed nine of 23 pass attempts for 145 yards, one touchdown and three interceptions. Sammy Baugh, meanwhile, only attempted five passes, completing four of them for 37 yards, one touchdown and no interceptions. The Redskins were leading 21-0 heading into the fourth quarter. Sid Luckman found halfback Ray McLean with a 58-yard pass and score to reduce the arrears.

'I would put Sammy Baugh as one of a number of great quarterbacks in NFL history,' Mike Richman told me.

'For his time, you can make an argument that he was the best. He played for 16 seasons from 1937 through 1952. I don't think anyone can argue he was one of the best quarterbacks during that era.'

Alongside Baugh and Sid Luckman as the greats of their time was the Brooklyn Dodgers' Ace Parker, who was serving with the Navy long before the 1943 NFL season began. 'Now, I think it is impossible to compare Sammy Baugh to the quarterbacks of today,' explained Richman. 'I think it is impossible to make that comparison because it was a totally different type of game. It was just a different era.

'When you talk about the greatest of all time, in any position, I would have to say Tom Brady is the greatest quarterback of all time, because who is going to top winning seven Super Bowls and playing for 20-plus seasons? I do not see that ever happening.

'Brady's era is a totally different game to the one that Sammy Baugh played in,' said Richman. Baugh developed into a truer quarterback from around 1944, during wartime. It was when the Redskins switched to the T-formation.

The T-formation had been around for years. It was the Bears who used it effectively in the NFL at that time. It is a basic concept, which separated the early inception of football as we know it from rugby. The design is when the quarterback lines up under centre, and the option can be to run to either side of the offence from this formation. Essentially, the quarterback became the centrepiece of this new offence, and the forward pass was the chief weapon.

The Redskins were victims of this in that 73-0 Championship loss in 1940. That one-sided demolition was the beacon of change for teams, especially Washington. Pittsburgh were reluctant to move from their single wing attack and did not change until the 1950s.

The T-formation lent itself to passing a lot better than offensive designs such as the old wing attacks. It allowed the quarterback to keep defences guessing each time he got the ball. Then, by turning his back to the line of scrimmage as soon as he got the snap, the quarterback disguised his intentions for the play from the defence. Those plans may have been a hand-off or pitch-out, but it delayed the opposition long enough for him to spot a receiver and make the pass.

The Bears' Sid Luckman was the first real superstar T-quarterback in the NFL. By the mid-1940s, Luckman's rival, Sammy Baugh, made the move. Of course, there was some pushback from football purists, who complained that the game was becoming too much like basketball because teams were throwing as many as 25 passes in a contest. Not everyone can be pleased all of the time.

As the two juggernauts prepared for another title showdown in 1943, the stakes were high. With war raging on foreign fields and fellow pros risking their lives for their country, Baugh and Luckman wanted to put on a show for the people at home to give them something to cheer while also maintaining pride with their respective teams.

Remember, this contest was being played on December 26; families had just spent Christmas unsure of the safety and wellbeing of loved ones in combat. There were no phone calls or WhatsApp messages offering season's greetings and assurances that they were safe and well.

More than 34,000 people packed into Chicago's Wrigley Field to watch the NFL's biggest rivals go at it once more with their superstars Baugh and Luckman. The game was tense to begin with and finished all square at 0-0 after the first quarter. Both defences had the upper hand in the early exchanges.

Washington took the lead near the start of the second quarter with a one-yard carry from running back Andy Farkas into the end zone. Sid Luckman answered almost immediately with a 31-yard touchdown pass to running back Harry Clarke. Clarke led the league in yards from scrimmage that season (1,091) and was All-Pro.

Before half-time Chicago had taken a 14-7 lead, courtesy of a touchdown run from their star fullback, Bronko Nagurski. At 6ft 2in and 235lb, Nagurski was an imposing figure darting out of the backfield, much like Derrick Henry of Alabama and the Tennessee Titans in the modern era. He also played tackle, as he was so big.

Nagurski was a two-time NFL champion with the Bears and had retired from football in 1937 to take up wrestling. He returned in 1943 to help the club because its roster had been so reduced by players fighting overseas. He was enshrined into the Pro Football Hall of Fame in 1963.

His go-ahead score for Chicago in the 1943 Championship Game gave the Bears a lead that they would not relinquish. After the interval Luckman took care of the rest. Having already thrown a touchdown pass in the first half, he threw four more in the second half. One of those was a 66-yard touchdown pass to running back Dante Magnani.

The Bears entered the fourth and final quarter with a 27-14 lead which they extended, thanks to Sid Luckman's arm, to an unassailable 41-14 advantage. Sammy Baugh threw a 25-yard pass to find the end zone, but it was a mere consolation as the Bears clinched the title 41-21.

Sid Luckman produced numbers in that game that will never be replicated. If Patrick Mahomes, Lamar Jackson, or Jalen Hurts were to do in the Super Bowl what Sid Luckman achieved in the 1943 Championship Game, they would immediately be crowned the Greatest of All Time by some people. Not only did he throw for 286 yards, five touchdowns and achieve a quarterback rating of 135.6, but he also led the game in rushing (64 yards). He outrushed the whole Redskins team combined. Luckman also intercepted two of Sammy Baugh's passes, which he returned for 33 yards. He returned two punts for 32 yards and even handled the punting duties, kicking three for 74 yards.

To this day, Sid Luckman holds NFL records from the 1943 season that have not been broken by any quarterback. He averaged the most passing yards per attempt in a single campaign (10.9 yards) and still maintains the best passing touchdown percentage (13.9) with 100-plus passing attempts in a single season.

During that MVP season of '43, Luckman also became the first player in history to throw for over 400 yards in a game. It was on the road against the New York Giants in Week 9. He completed 21 of 32 pass attempts for 433 yards and a record-equalling seven touchdown passes. Only seven other players have achieved that number of scoring passes in a game in NFL history. The most recent was Drew Brees, against the Giants, in 2015.

It can be argued that those numbers are inflated due to fewer games being played that season. Luckman faced a poorer standard of opposition because so many top professionals stepped away from the league to fight in the Second World War. However, his team was also depleted and some of the offensive plays would have been simplified to help ringers adapt to the offence. This was a time when American football was very much run-heavy. It was light years from the athletic passing spectacle that it is today, making Luckman's achievements even more impressive.

The year Luckman began his college career at Columbia University in 1936, his father, Meyer Luckman, was convicted of second-degree murder for beating his wife's brother to death. Sid spoke little about his father's conviction but would visit him in prison.

After his record '43 season with the Chicago Bears ended, Luckman volunteered as an ensign with the Merchant Marines. He was stationed in the States and was allowed to play for the Bears, although he was not given permission to practise with the team.

Months before the following season, Luckman discovered that his father was suffering from a heart condition. He appealed for him to be released from prison on compassionate grounds but that was denied. Meyer Luckman died in January 1944.

The other poster boy of the league in 1943, Sammy Baugh, was making records of his own. Like Peyton Manning and Tom Brady 60 years later, Baugh and Luckman were the two stars who were playing at a different level to their competition.

This was the era of platoon football; therefore players had to operate in multiple positions. Baugh was extremely versatile, and he ended the campaign as the NFL leader in passing, pass interceptions (on defence), and punting. In the game against the Detroit Lions on November 14, 1943, Baugh made four defensive interceptions. It is a record that has never been broken. Nineteen players have equalled it in 79 seasons since.

The Washington Commanders' website has a page dedicated to 'Slingin' Sammy', and on it is a quote from the Hall of Fame quarterback, Ace Parker, who said, 'He was the best passer I ever saw. He could do everything. He could pass, he could play defence, he was the best kicker, and he still holds the single season punting record [in 1940].' The punting record (51.4 yards per punt) was broken in 2022 by the Tennessee Titans punter, Ryan Stonehouse (53.1

yards per punt). Stonehouse did not also play quarterback or defensive back.

Only Drew Brees has led the NFL in passing (seven seasons) more often than Sammy Baugh (six seasons).

***

Sid Luckman played seven of ten games in '44 and the Bears missed out on the Championship Game, finishing second in the Western Conference behind the Green Bay Packers. Despite his limited game time, Luckman was awarded his fourth consecutive First Team All-Pro selection.

The NFL continued to be impacted by the war in that 1944 season. The Philadelphia Eagles chose to part ways with the Pittsburgh Steelers, thus ending the brief Steagles run. It is believed that the two coaches could not stand the thought of having to work with each other for another year.

Following their brief hiatus, the Cleveland Rams returned to the league. There was also a new team in the competition. Owner Ted Collins was awarded a franchise for Boston. So, the 1944 season saw the introduction of the Boston Yanks. He had intended on having a franchise at Yankee Stadium in New York.

There was also a new name for the Brooklyn Dodgers that year. They became known as the Brooklyn Tigers. Meanwhile, the Steelers, still severely impacted by the war effort, merged with the Chicago Cardinals. The team was officially known as the Car-Pitt Combine. Fans quickly called them the Carpets, in reference to how bad they were. They were the doormats of the league because everyone was walking all over them.

The Car-Pitts went 0-10 that season. They struggled on defence, and the fewest points they conceded in a game was 21, which came in a 21-7 defeat to the Detroit Lions in

Week 9. However, they were not the only team to suffer the indignity of an 0-10 record in 1944. The toothless Brooklyn Tigers had a purr, rather than a roar, losing every game. No team lost all their games in a single season again until 32 years later in 1976, when the newly formed Tampa Bay Buccaneers went 0-14 in their debut season (they lost their first 26 games in the NFL).

A full losing season has only been achieved twice more. The Detroit Lions went 0-16 in 2008. Coached by Rod Marinelli, they lost by 10 or more points in 11 games that year. The Lions gave up 517 points to their opponents, who averaged 32.3 points per game. Offensively, the Lions scored a grand total of 268 points in 2008, an average of 16.8 points per game. They did all of this with Calvin Johnson as their second-year wide receiver. Despite their lacklustre performances that season, Johnson recorded 1,331 receiving yards and 12 touchdowns.

The last team to have a campaign with no wins or a tie was the 2017 Cleveland Browns. Led by Hue Jackson, the Browns scored a total of 234 points, averaging 14.6 points per game. This was the fewest points scored in the modern era. Defensively, they weren't as bad as the 2008 Lions. The Browns gave up 410 points in 2017. They lost six games by a touchdown or less and went to overtime against the Green Bay Packers and Tennessee Titans. Their campaign ended 0-16.

As for the war-torn Car-Pitts, the Pittsburgh Steelers owner, Art Rooney, said 30 years later, 'That was the worst team ever. The Steagles were world beaters compared to that team.' That was before the Tampa Bay Buccaneers had ever kicked a ball.

The Redskins and the Bears continued to have the better passing offences in 1944, but neither team topped their respective conferences. Both clubs had 6-3-1 seasons.

With the league's top two teams out of the playoffs, the Championship Game was contested between the Green Bay Packers and New York Giants. The Packers won 14-7 on December 17.

Throughout the Second World War, professional football was still below baseball in terms of popularity. The National Football League was just beginning to get a decent national following, thanks to the likes of Luckman, Baugh, and Ace Parker. If there was a team in their city, national newspapers would report on games. Coverage was thinner in states with smaller towns and cities because there was not that much interest in the National Football League. Those regions had their local college football, which preserved their engagement and support.

But as the war began, and eventually rolled on, college football suffered terribly because as many as 200 teams disappeared. In 1943 most colleges did not play at all. Those that were playing only managed to participate on a very limited schedule and mostly played certain states, rather than other colleges or universities.

Although the National Football League was growing during the early to mid-1940s, it did not have the following of college football or 'America's pastime', baseball. However, with crowds in their tens of thousands, it was certainly developing public interest. It had started building fan bases in the 1930s, especially towards the end of that decade, but the war halted its engagement.

The Second World War was a real detriment to the development of the National Football League due to the exodus of talent. Teams like the Car-Pitts and Steagles, though they helped keep the league operational, did not do much for the product on show. The quality of football was poorer throughout the league. Which, again, highlights how important it was to have stars such as Luckman and Baugh around during that era.

CHAPTER 20

The United Service Organizations

'There were lots of stops and so many interactions, and the NFL guys could not get enough of it'

– NFL Media presenter, Marc Sessler

THERE WOULD not have been a Tea Bowl or Coffee Bowl without the presence of a United Service Organizations (USO) representative sitting in that London pub in December 1943.

It was the USO who had provided the football equipment that the serviceman whom Denis Whitaker encountered claimed was 'enough to field six teams'. At that time the institution was in its infancy.

In 1941, before the United States entered the Second World War, President Franklin D. Roosevelt wanted to create a support group for the country's armed forces. He wanted to bring together the Salvation Army, Young Men's Christian Association (YMCA), the Young Women's Christian Association (YWCA), the National Catholic Community Service, the National Travelers Aid Association, and the National Jewish Welfare Board.

By February 4 of that year, those six organisations formed the USO. Their purpose? To provide morale and recreation services to the troops.

When Pearl Harbor was attacked and America entered World War II, the USO immediately sprang into operation, ensuring the forces that the organisation was by their side. Troops were beginning to mobilise in their hundreds of thousands, therefore the USO began building a network of centres across the United States. Those centres were constructed for recreational use, and were formed from churches, stores, museums, barns – whatever space they could find that would provide a place of comfort and support for servicemen.

At those centres, as well as at military bases, the USO provided its members with high-end entertainment throughout the Second World War, including top shows from the likes of Laurel and Hardy, Bob Hope, and Glenn Miller.

Miller became a tragic victim of the war. On December 15, 1944, he boarded an Eighth Air Force Service Command Norseman aircraft at the RAF Twinwood aerodrome, Clapham, Bedfordshire. The plane was heading for Ninth Air Force aerodrome, Velizy-Villacoublay in France.

Miller, whose hits included 'Moonlight Serenade' and 'In the Mood', was on his way to organise a Christmas concert for the troops in liberated Paris. His jazz trombonist was with him.

Their plane disappeared over the English Channel, and was ever seen or heard from again. After the plane's disappearance, the Eighth Air Force launched a search and investigation, eventually determining that the likely causes were pilot disorientation, mechanical failure, or bad weather. Neither the plane nor any of the people on board have ever been found.

The USO was more than entertainment. It provided a safe space for troops where they could write letters to their families. They were also coffee shops and even places where people could go to rest.

Out on the front line, where young men found themselves far from home, alone, and in strange lands, many never having left home before, the USO brought the troops a taste of America. Top stars would appear at camps in France and put on shows. It was not just in Europe where these camp shows toured. Performances were seen in North Africa, the Middle East, and the Pacific.

The USO website, uso.org, has a quote from Bob Hope in 1944: 'Believe me when I say that laughter up at the front lines is a very precious thing – precious to those grand guys who are giving and taking the awful business that goes on there.' Hope travelled the world to perform and boost morale for the servicemen fighting on all fronts.

During the peak of the Second World War, the USO estimated that one million service members were served each day. By the end of World War II, the USO had put on more than 300,000 performances with nearly 5,000 entertainers.

During the Korean War, Marilyn Monroe travelled on tour to support the troops who had been deployed. Bob Hope continued touring, and in 1964 performed a Christmas show in Vietnam with a host of special guests, including the NFL's Rosey Grier. By this point, football was overtaking baseball as the number one sport in America.

In 2010, the late Robin Williams flew to Bagram in Afghanistan and left American service personnel in stitches with his brilliant brand of humour and comedy.

But the organisation does more than put on shows for troops. It has remained true to its roots of being a place of comfort and sometimes solace. With the NFL it has allowed servicemen and women to get close to the stars they worship from afar.

Many of the players and coaches that travel to be with them have military links in their families and understand the importance of these visits.

And that's what they are. They are not trips, nor are they celebrity tours. They are visits. Each player and coach that travels understands the value of their visit and they invest their time in the people they meet. That sense of team and the regimented structure to their daily lives creates a bond between the two groups.

In 2018, Marc Sessler, a successful American football presenter, co-host from the popular *Around the NFL* podcast, and reporter for NFL Media, was sent to Italy and Germany with football players and a coach to share his experience of the league's visit to USO centres abroad.

'What I saw, specifically on those European trips was that we brought a gang of players, it was Mark Ingram, Latavius Murray, Mario Addison, Carlos Dunlap, Ben Garland, and Rex Ryan,' Sessler told me. 'And I think it was really important [those individuals were selected], because it wasn't just "Oh, let's get any NFL players to go."' This was because a few of the NFL personalities he was with had military connections.

The NFL and USO have a partnership that goes back more than 50 years. It's part of an effort to strengthen service members and their families by connecting them to family, home, and country, regardless of where they are around the world.

'On our visit,' said Sessler, 'in many cases, the NFL guys I was with had military ties. They had at least some sort of connection from a family angle to the military, where there was probably a perspective of understanding of the sacrifices these military families would make.'

Carlos Dunlap is the son of two military veterans. Ben Garland attended Air Force at college and played for the Air Force Falcons. At the time of his visit in 2018, Garland had played in two Super Bowls and fulfilled his military duties between NFL seasons.

'So, together we flew out to these bases in Europe,' Marc explained. 'And I knew right away that we brought the right group of people because we'd be on a bus, then you get off and you go. It's then full-on, you would spend an hour and a half or two hours with the service people you're visiting.'

The bases that Sessler and the NFL stars visited were deep in Italy and Germany. A lot of the people they were meeting were young. Many were without their families. Also, they could be called into action at any moment. Therefore, there is a semi-permanent feeling of anxiety looming over them.

Although they were in the company of other soldiers, these young people admitted to Marc and the players that there could be a sense of loneliness at times. But that loneliness dissipated when the NFL arrived.

'You would just see the place light up,' said Marc, 'the minute that this group of players and Coach Ryan stepped off the bus and would meet them.

'We did this every day. There were lots of stops and so many interactions, and the NFL guys could not get enough of it. They knew how important it was to these people we were visiting, and they made sure each individual received the time and respect they deserved.'

Marc explained how he could see that some of the soldiers were in awe of the players they were meeting. These were the superstars lighting up their TVs when they got to watch sports. Many of them likely had Mark Ingram and Latavius Murray on their fantasy football teams. Suddenly these players were just like one of them, spending time in their company and hanging out. It was unlike an ordinary day on camp with a longing for home. The best of home was with them, interacting and paying an interest.

The players were personable, sharing lunch and dinner with the troops. Mark Ingram spent time playing the Madden video game with whoever would take him on. Perhaps even a day earlier, one of the servicemen or women had been Ingram on that video game, and now he was sat next to them playing it as though he was one of their friends.

As Marc said, 'I came away with this appreciation that back here [at home], you are just doing whatever you're doing. But at all times, there are these bases filled with soldiers, many of whom are so young, that at any moment can be thrown into war. But that particular moment in time was like a little bit of a change of pace. And I think the USO always was kind of like, "Let's lift them around, let's do something special. Let's remind you that we haven't forgotten about you back in the States."'

During an NFL offseason, hundreds of millionaire athletes find themselves with time on their hands. An American football season is brutally demanding on the body and mind. The time afforded to rest and recuperate is well earned. These athletes, therefore, have the freedom to travel the world and experience things that the average person cannot. They also do a lot of travelling throughout the season, flying from city to city, often cross-country, for work. So, travelling to the middle of Europe in the spring was nothing new to this group.

Marc told me how they arrived in Venice straight off a flight from the States and were full of energy. There was a youthful enthusiasm to explore the city and experience its culture. Those energy levels remained high when they were in the presence of service personnel. The players and Coach Ryan brought a spark and engagement to each and every person they met.

'We got to the base,' said Marc, 'and it was not like they felt that they had to be serious because they were in the company of soldiers. The players had immense respect, but they brought their personalities with them. They really engaged and wanted to know everything about the soldiers they were talking to.'

Very similar to the military, the NFL is a well-oiled machine. The USO had people who ensured the talent on show were punctual. It was a regimen that suited the NFL stars. A special bond was forming with each stop made, as players and troops shared stories and experiences.

The troops were immediately humbled by how relatable the players were. There is a viral video of Mark Ingram running from a guard dog in protective clothing and being thrown to the ground as if he was a Pop Warner back being tackled by Aaron Donald. He was not forced to do that and did it out of choice. In doing so, he made a connection and proved he was not above the soldiers because of his millionaire status. He remained grounded; they all did. Mark Ingram personified the United Service Organizations in that he brought support and a morale boost through his actions.

It was not a visit about shaking hands, smiling, and looking engaged for the camera. These players cared. They were selected for a reason. The USO has been supporting troops for more than 80 years. The players are far removed from the early hostesses who dressed up in the dance halls in the 1940s and danced with lonely soldiers who had no one around them. But the same form of care is still there. Rex Ryan, a former head coach of multiple NFL franchises, sat and ate with people as if he was one of them, talking like a father and engaging in conversation.

The USO made a point that at each stop, every soldier would have a chance to interact. And at those stops each player gave them the same level of focus and engagement. From a physical standpoint, these players had met their match with the soldiers. Competitions took place between NFL stars and troops from flipping tractor tyres to obstacle races. No matter how lonely they were feeling, those soldiers were gifted a moment where they could say they got to take on a Heisman Trophy winner and might even say that they beat him. The players and USO were fulfilling their promise. Everyone had an eagerness to dive right in for their hosts.

'I saw in person why the people they brought were very relatable and great at what they did,' Marc Sessler said. 'I think you have someone like Rex Ryan, who is a natural leader. And the guys we were with were also all natural leaders. They were the leaders of their high school and college teams, the best athletes on those teams and at the centre of everything. Therefore, that part of their personalities related with soldiers who had similar accountability and leadership.'

There were many NFL tours with the USO before Marc Sessler's trip with Ryan, Dunlap, Garland, Ingram and Murray in 2018. Hall of Fame quarterback Terry Bradshaw is one of countless football stars to visit troops abroad.

As an organisation, the USO puts on Super Bowl watch parties for troops. The bases are filled with young people, staying up until three or four o'clock in the morning to watch the biggest American spectacle. Suddenly they get the opportunity, not just to meet some of those stars from the televised games, but also to spend time with them and hang out as if they are buddies.

'It's like, if you asked them who they would rather have, a pop star on tour or a bunch of NFL players? I think the NFL players would get a lot of votes,' Marc summarised.

'And so, I think that there was this natural connection and understanding between the day-to-day mechanics of being on base, where you have very defined activities with some free time in there, and the same for the NFL player. I think that there's this realisation of, it's not more for football. Obviously, the players are preparing for an opponent on a weekly basis and even in the offseason they're preparing themselves, but I think there's a lot of links between all that.'

'Therefore, it's different than if you brought a rock band that's smoking and drinking to play for the soldiers. The NFL players and coaches had nuances to the troops.'

Superstars like Andrew Luck have travelled with the USO to meet with soldiers around the world. The former Indianapolis Colts quarterback, who was one of the most talented players to come out of college, is the son of the ex-Houston Oilers quarterback, Oliver Luck.

Oliver explained to me how his son felt a sense of duty to take a taste of home to the troops that he met. These were people who had been sent halfway around the world to protect their country. It was not a holiday for them. Many were stationed at bases in the middle of nowhere, away from any form of culture and without the conveniences readily available in urban dwellings.

Andrew helped bring a taste of America and light entertainment. He lifted their spirits. There was normalcy, no matter how brief, and that provided a boost to morale. Just as Marc Sessler witnessed in 2018.

With Andrew Luck, the soldiers had one of the biggest quarterbacks in the league in their company. The former number one overall NFL draft pick was taking a genuine interest in their work. They had a mutual respect and as he left, they had become equally motivated.

CHAPTER 21

The NFL and the Armed Forces

'There clearly was a pretty significant impact played by former American soldiers'

– ex-Houston Oilers quarterback, and former head of NFL Europe, Oliver Luck

THE NATIONAL Football League's relationship with the armed forces dates back more than half a century. American football is a sport where opponents fight for territory. Terms such as 'trenches', 'blitzes' and 'bombs' are used in every game that is played. It is seemingly natural for football and the military to co-exist.

There is a massive sense of patriotism around the American football experience. 'The Star-Spangled Banner' is passionately sung by tens of thousands of spectators before each game. The United States flag covers the field, generating immense pride as fighter jets fly overhead. Football is primarily played on a Sunday, the sacred day when families get together, go to church, then gather round the television to eat and cheer on their teams.

In 1960, the National Football League appointed a new commissioner who would elevate the sport to number one in America. The commissioner they appointed was a 'compromise candidat' because the owners could not agree on who they wanted. That compromise turned out to be the revolutionary that built the foundations for the NFL as we know it today.

Pete Rozelle was a visionary. At the time of his appointment, televisions were becoming permanent fixtures in households across the country. Only a few teams had broadcasting rights, and their 12-game schedules were uninspiring.

Rozelle structured a deal that would allow profit-sharing of television and gate revenues. This meant teams in smaller markets than the metropolises of New York, Chicago and Washington could have a fighting chance.

The new commissioner had served with the Navy during the Second World War and toured in the Pacific. Following the war, Rozelle worked in the publicity department for the league's first California team, the Los Angeles Rams. The Rams had moved west in 1946 from Cleveland. Pete Rozelle was a freshman at Compton Junior College, where the team practised. By the time he graduated in 1950, Rozelle was assistant athletic director but landed his full-time PR position with the franchise two years later.

Six years into his tenure, Rozelle oversaw the merger of the AFL and the NFL. It was 1966 and he knew that the National Football League needed the merger if it was to continue to evolve. The two leagues united to become one in 1970. The first Super Bowl, billed as the AFL-NFL World Championship game, took place in Los Angeles in January 1967.

The following year, Rozelle introduced the first ever pre-game military flyover. In doing so, he set up a relationship with the Department of Defense that would last for decades. Military aircraft continue their flyovers during the national anthem at the Super Bowl. The 1969 showpiece had a theme called 'America Thanks' as its half-time pageant, with the commissioner keen on harnessing patriotism and football.

Rozelle once said, 'It was a conscious effort on our part to bring the element of patriotism into the Super Bowl.'

A few years before the first Super Bowl, Rozelle had started sending players on tour with the USO, not only to boost morale but also the league's image as it gave thanks and heartfelt acknowledgement to the service personnel.

Super Bowl Sunday is an unofficial holiday for the whole of the United States of America. It is a unified celebration of sport and nationalism. Patriotism is at its heart. In 1991, the NFL's commissioner, Paul Tagliabue said, 'We've become the winter version of the Fourth of July celebration.'

In the autumn of 2001, weeks after the United States was attacked during 9/11, President George W. Bush announced that the country had gone to war in Afghanistan. The announcement was made on a Sunday morning, which was also an NFL game day. That day, Bush's speech was relayed on giant screens inside football stadiums, the pantheons for patriotism.

The Super Bowl in 2002, which ended that 2001 season that had begun so tragically, featured a three-hour pre-game show on Fox. *Heroes, Hope, and Homeland* culminated with a 'Tribute to America', featuring ex-NFL players reading from the Declaration of Independence. This Super Bowl had the famous U2 half-time show, with the names of the victims of 9/11 appearing on the screen at the end of the band's performance.

Navy destroyers and aircraft carriers were visited by the Fox TV crew for the Super Bowls in 2003 and 2005, with the country at war in Iraq and Afghanistan.

* * *

Since 2011, the National Football League has raised more than $66 million for military causes through its Salute to Service campaigns. The league has generated the money by selling specially designed camouflage Salute to Service merchandise. Proceeds from the sales are donated to non-profits, along with other charities. Its partnerships are with the Bob Woodruff Foundation (BWF), Pat Tillman Foundation (PTF), Tragedy Assistance Program for Survivors (TAPS), United Service Organizations (USO) and Wounded Warrior Project® (WWP).

The NFL has three main objectives in its commitment to the military community: to honour, empower, and connect. According to its official website, the league honours the service and sacrifice of the American military through partnerships, grants, and recognition of service members, veterans, and their families.

For empowerment, the league leverages its platform and resources to create a positive impact for America's heroes. In collaboration with the NFL's partners, the league works on enhancing the independence of wounded warriors, improving veteran's physical and mental health, and promoting prosperity within the military community.

And to connect, the NFL unites service members and their families through a shared love of football, fostering connections within the military community and beyond.

One of the main commercial partners with the NFL is the USAA. Known as the United Services Automobile Association, the USAA is the official NFL Salute to Service partner. It is an American financial services company that provides insurance and banking products exclusively to members of the military, veterans, and their families. On multiple occasions during game day broadcasts, prominent NFL figures such as the former New England Patriots and Tampa Bay Buccaneers tight end, Rob Gronkowski, appear on commercials for their services.

The USAA has its name attached to one of the league's major awards, which is presented annually at the NFL Honors during Super Bowl week. The award is the Salute to Service Award and acknowledges the exceptional efforts by members of the NFL community to honour and support US service members, veterans, and their families. Winners include Ron Rivera, Andrew Beck, Steve Cannon, and Ben Garland.

In November 2023, the San Francisco 49ers tight end George Kittle was nominated for the award. Speaking at a press conference, Kittle explained the pride he felt in being shortlisted for the honour: 'The military, it means a lot to me. I have family members who have served, I've seen the toll it takes on families when they're overseas,' said Kittle. 'And they're gone from their families, I've seen that in real life, I've got a chance to work with wonderful organisations like TAPS [Tragedy Assistance Program for Survivors], merging vets and players, Operation Freedom Paws [a non-profit organisation that connects service dogs to veterans and individuals with disabilities].

'Every time I get a chance to work with a military family, or just an organisation, all I can be is just thankful, because these are people who sacrifice everything, from the person who is serving to their entire family. A lot of them give the ultimate sacrifice for this country. And because of them, we're allowed to all do this, I get to play a football game, you guys get to report on a football game. And we don't have to worry about that stuff, really. So, I'm always just so thankful of them. And I just don't feel like our military gets enough support and recognition all the time. And so, I'm very happy to be part of the NFL who does a great job, and I wish it was year-long, but we give them a month and to be able to bring a bunch of veterans to football games weekly for me and my family, it always means a lot just trying to give back to them as much as we possibly can.'

During his final season in the league, the seven-time Super Bowl champion, Tom Brady, faced a backlash from veterans of the US armed forces when he compared playing on the gridiron to life in the service.

Speaking on his *Let's Go! with Tom Brady, Larry Fitzgerald and Jim Gray* podcast, Brady, whom many believe to be the greatest football player of all time, said, 'I almost look at a football season like you're going away on deployment in the military, and it's like, "Man, here I go again."'

A veteran tagged Brady on social media and reminded him that the late Arizona Cardinals defender, Pat Tillman, waived a multi-million-dollar NFL contract to join the US Army Rangers in 2002, following the 9/11 terror attacks. Tillman died of friendly fire in 2004. He was a year older than Brady.

'I really, really, REALLY hope Tom Brady gives a public apology for his ignorant remarks,' tweeted combat veteran, Alberto Romero. 'I'm sure Mr Pat Tillman would not agree with him.'

Army veteran, Brad Thomas, who fought in Black Hawk Down, shared his anger at Brady on Instagram. 'Hey @ tombrady – this statement is naïve and offensive on many levels,' wrote Thomas. 'You play a game, for entertainment, and seem to have lost your perspective.'

A few days later, at the start of the quarterback's weekly pre-game press conference, Tom Brady interrupted a reporter whilst standing at the podium and issued an apology. 'I have a tremendous amount of gratitude for everyone who served,' said Brady. 'And, in the end, we play a game, and the military is defending our country. It's two different things and I shouldn't have made the comparison.'

The Buccaneers were on the road to play their NFC South division rivals, the Carolina Panthers, that week and lost 21-3. Brady threw for 290 yards, zero touchdowns and zero interceptions. Tampa Bay's only points came from a field goal in the fourth quarter.

Three weeks later, Brady and the Buccaneers were in Germany as the home team for the first-ever NFL regular season game in the country. They faced the Seattle Seahawks on November 13, 2022, and during the game the NFL brought three women on to the field for the crowd to salute. The women were from Ukraine. Their husbands were American football players defending their country against the Russian invasion. It was a display of the NFL's recognition of bravery. This recognition was publicly presented in central Europe, rather than the United States, and out of respect to the conflict affecting the lives of people on the continent where the league was being hosted. Tom Brady met the Ukrainian families after the game. He shared a picture with them on his Instagram page and called them heroes.

The NFL recognised British armed forces at its London games in 2014, when the Jacksonville Jaguars hosted the Dallas Cowboys at Wembley Stadium, on Remembrance Sunday. The league teamed up with the Royal British Legion to raise money for its Poppy Appeal. Giant poppies were on display with fans asked to hold up cards that were assigned to their seats. British troops were honoured throughout the game, much as teams do with servicemen and women in the States, and money raised from the auction of game day uniforms went to the UK charity.

In 2023, the National Football League returned to Germany and hosted two games in Frankfurt. Ahead of the first game, the Miami Dolphins linebacker, Jaelan Phillips, told reporters during a press conference that he had been to Germany as a child because his aunt was stationed there with the military. Phillips has a strong connection with the US armed forces, more so than most of his peers in the NFL. Given his family relationship with the military, I asked him if he thought the league's long-standing relationship with the armed forces is important.

'Oh, I think it's super important,' Phillips said. 'Obviously, giving credit where credit is due, the people who risk their lives protecting our countries, I think it's important to give them the respect they deserve. I think there's actually about 35 active military personnel coming to the game [Miami Dolphins vs. Kansas City Chiefs] that my aunt's friends with. To be able to see them after the game and just acknowledge them, like I said, is going to be really important.'

Ahead of the first ever NFL game in Frankfurt, I had the opportunity to speak with the leading American football sportswriter, Peter King. King wrote for *Sports Illustrated* for 29 years and is recognized worldwide for the 'Monday Morning Quarterback' column he wrote. He writes the 'Football Morning in America' column each week for NBC.

Speaking about the National Football League's working relationship with the military, King said, 'I think a lot of it has to do with the fact that so many people, and so many people in the United States who joined the military, and who end up serving overseas, become huge advocates for the NFL.

'There is a big population of armed forces personnel here in Germany. A lot of these people become huge fans, wherever they are in the world, and are huge advocates of football.

'But I also think that has something to do with the two disciplines, because they are very similar. It even goes down to the vocabulary involved, such as blitz, trenches, and things like that. So, I just think there's a lot of that. And I also think that over time, there has been an aligning. People in the military, generals, and influencers from the armed forces. They love football. It's a tough game. It's a physical game. And I'm sure that a lot of their best soldiers over the years have come from football. Therefore, there is a lot of relativity between the sport of football and the military.'

Former Houston Oilers quarterback Oliver Luck worked in Frankfurt during the early 1990s as general manager of the Frankfurt Galaxy. The very first amateur American football team in Europe were the Frankfurter Lowen, or Frankfurt Lions.

The sport had been played recreationally in parts of western Europe by American troops stationed there throughout the Cold War. The Frankfurt Lions were set up by Alexander Sperber, Wolfgang Lehneis and Dieter Heil in 1976. They played exhibition games but were generating an interest in the area. The pollination of American football and the US military was growing the shoots of the sport internationally.

American forces personnel had brought their game to foreign soil. By the early 1990s the sport was so big, the NFL decided to set up a team there and sent one of its former players to lead the way.

'Whether it's the UK or Germany, American football grabbed on to some grass, if you will, in places that were strongly influenced by the US military,' Oliver Luck told me over a cup of coffee in the centre of Frankfurt on the eve of the first NFL regular season game in the city.

'And you don't have to know too much history to know that after the war the Brits pretty much took northern Germany as its occupation zone,' Luck added. 'So, if you get stuck, the East basically, the Americans took Bavaria and Baden Wurttemberg, and has some of the south. And, you know, people forget, we had a lot of troops over here.'

Throughout the Cold War, there were about 500,000 Americans, half of which were troops, in south and south-west Germany. On top of that were the tens of thousands of civilian employees of the Department of Defense, where the American military had taken over existing German

Wehrmacht installations, which were the country's armed forces bases.

'When I first came over in the late 80s, early 90s, it was just as the Berlin Wall was coming down,' Oliver said, 'and the withdrawal of American troops didn't really happen until around 1992–93, when the people realised that the Soviet Union wasn't a threat. But, prior to that, there were a lot of troops who stayed in Germany because they married German women. These guys began the foundations of little clubs that started to pop up, because they liked football. That was their game. Some of them had kids and they wanted to coach them American football. Be the proud dad, which is a desire of lots of parents.'

In some instances, this also provided a way for these troops to give back to the community that had taken them in. 'So, there's a whole history and those guys, most of who are now old or dead because they were probably 40 back in the 1970s and 1980s, those former servicemen decided to stay in Germany, and along with a few others, started to get the game of American football going.

'And this is something that is harder for a lot of Europeans to understand because America is defined by race, while Europe is defined by class,' Luck explained. 'The British have struggled with class. They do pretty well on the race stuff. But they struggle with class. Americans, meanwhile, we struggle with the race stuff. We do very well on class.

'So, football is this crazy game where, you can have privileged kids, my son [former Indianapolis Colts quarterback Andrew Luck] grew up as a privileged kid. But you can be in a locker room, be respected by kids who grew up in tough economic circumstances, rural poverty or whatever. Therefore, it cuts through football and cuts through most of our sports. It also cuts through all of our socio-economic divisions really well.'

Relating what Oliver Luck was explaining about the military, there had been former officers in the local German towns, also throughout Europe and the United Kingdom. These towns also homed privates who, just like their officers, were half the world away from the homes they knew in the United States. What bonded these officers and privates? American football. They all got together and said, 'We like football, this is our game.' There was no class divide.

Luck shared an interesting reflection as we sat opposite one another inside the hotel breakfast lounge, sipping coffees. There were lots of Americans around and the Kansas City Chiefs were being accommodated there. 'I have often thought,' Luck said, 'what would have happened had there not been World War Two? Would the game be as big as it is today? You can't rewrite history but there clearly was a pretty significant impact played by former American soldiers.'

Oliver had lived in Frankfurt and has spent a lot of time in Germany. American football has been a huge part of his family's life. He was a quarterback. His son, Andrew, was the first-overall pick in the 2012 NFL draft. Just as Oliver's family had moved to Europe when he was appointed to his various roles with the World League of American Football and NFL Europe, Oliver followed Andrew to Indianapolis when he was drafted by the Colts.

For that weekend in early November, 2023, Oliver was back in Frankfurt to see the city that had welcomed him 32 years earlier, and he was experiencing first-hand the growth of the sport that he helped introduce to the area.

He had every right to feel reflective because the National Football League and its reigning Super Bowl champions, including their MVP quarterback, were in town. If in 1990, Oliver had suggested the San Francisco 49ers and Joe Montana took one of their home games against a main NFC rival to Germany, or even London, he would have been reconsidered for his position. But American football has grown so popular, thanks partly to US troops stationed around the world, that the NFL's commissioner, Roger Goodell, announced in December 2023 that the league and its owners had agreed to double its international schedule from four to eight games in 2025. Marketing rights have been issued to teams on every continent, citing global growth as a major strategic priority.

'One of the great clubs in German amateur history was the Berlin Adler, the Berlin Eagles,' Luck told me. 'And it is no surprise because Berlin as a city was divided up into the various zones. All the American guys that were in Berlin, and there was a lot of them, they got the game started. They began teaching German kids how to play the game of American football.

'So that's a pretty cool story that hasn't really been chronicled or researched. But it is a fact, because the game has a much different sort of history in Germany than it did in France. But even in France, I remember reading the story about the first American football game that ever took place there. Again, it was soldiers in the south of France in 1909.'

What Luck was referencing was the Great White Fleet. The Fleet was part of the US Navy and had been sent around the world by President Theodore Roosevelt from late 1907 to February 1909. It consisted of 16 battleships of the Atlantic Fleet. The battleships were painted white.

Nearly a decade later, American troops in France were sent helmets and footballs as part of their recreational supplies during the First World War. Soldiers would play games, but not in front of the capacity crowds witnessed in World War II.

Peter King feels assured that the National Football League and the United States armed forces have a connection that will continue for decades to come. 'I would think so,' he said. 'Because the NFL will be around to stay, the military will be around to stay.

'There is no doubt about that because the game has a lot of the life lessons that people in the military want to be their lessons,' King summarised. 'It is the same thing. It's hard work, plus you do the little things. They are both disciplines. Both are very, very disciplined things. And I just think that the people who are leaders in football love the military, the people who are leaders in the military love football. So, I think there is always going to be that connection.'

CHAPTER 22

Pat Tillman

'I never asked him why he decided to do it because I knew he had reasons, legitimate reasons. And his team-mates were the same way'

– Dave McGinnis, head coach of the Arizona Cardinals 2000–03

PAT TILLMAN was much like all the brave football players who had participated in the Tea Bowl and Coffee Bowl games. He felt a strong sense of duty to serve his country during a time of conflict. Unlike those heroes from World War II, Tillman did not have to serve, and he had a sports contract that was worth millions of dollars. There was also a bigger playing contract on its way to him.

The next few pages are dedicated to Pat Tillman, as told through his former head coach, Dave McGinnis. Dave knew Pat better than most outside of the Tillman family. He spoke with Pat when the NFL star chose to pause his career to fight for what he believed was right. There are political controversies linked to the treatment of Pat Tillman and the National Football League. Circumstances around Pat's tragic death and its reporting have been called into question. This chapter does not go into that.

I have chosen to focus on Pat Tillman the football player because his story synchronises with those gallant football players who had been willing to risk everything for freedom 60 years prior. War is terrible. Denis Whitaker did not want it, nor did Tommy Thompson, Jeff Nicklin, and neither did Pat Tillman.

This book is a non-fiction sports book about two football games that were played during a time of conflict and its aim is to share the stories of some of those brilliant men involved.

The circumstances for those men were different to the millionaire sports star who could have continued playing if he wanted to. He had already become a hero through his performances on the field. This is for Pat.

* * *

The former Arizona Cardinals safety is regarded as the ultimate American hero. He is an NFL legend, immortalised in league and Arizona sporting history.

Tillman was drafted by the Cardinals in 1998. Their defensive coordinator, Dave McGinnis, was aware of his talents, having watched him at Arizona State University in Tempe. 'I had been involved in drafting Pat Tillman,' Coach McGinnis told me when we met in London. 'When I was still the defensive coordinator at Arizona, I went and worked him out. We just loved him. The Sun Devils had gone to the Rose Bowl, they had Jake Plummer at quarterback, as well as Pat. That college team was a really good football team. Pat Tillman was the PAC-10 Defensive Player of the Year, and he was an undersized player. But he had defied all odds.'

He was given the last scholarship at Arizona State. The late Bruce Snyder was the head coach when Tillman arrived at the Sun Devils and he told Pat that he was going to redshirt him for his first season. Pat Tillman was having none of it and demanded there was no way it would happen. 'He said "No Coach, you're not,"' McGinnis recalled. 'Pat told Snyder that he had things to do with his life and he had three and a half years to give to the Arizona State Sun Devils.'

'He was brilliant,' Dave McGinnis said. 'Just brilliant.'

It was because of his size that Pat Tillman slid through the rounds of the NFL draft in 1998. The Arizona Cardinals wanted him, and they made sure that they got him, albeit late in the seventh round. As soon as he arrived at Cardinals headquarters, Tillman immediately made an impression on his coaches. 'Pat came to see me quite early on when he joined us,' explained Coach McGinnis.

'He sat down, like you and I are talking right now, and said, "Hey, Coach, I know why you drafted me. I'm a local kid who will put some more people in the stands. You think I'll probably be a good special team player."'

Tillman laid it all out there for his new coach. He asked that McGinnis spend time with him so he could prove that he was good enough to be the Cardinals' starting safety. This was a 22-year-old just days into his first professional football contract and he was already instructing his coordinator to give him a chance. He had that much confidence in his ability.

'And I went, "Okay. I will." And I did.'

Pat Tillman was as advertised. By the start of the 1998 season, he was the starting safety for the Arizona Cardinals. He started 10 of 16 games in his rookie season but featured in all 16. Tillman recorded a sack, had a pass deflection, and made 46 tackles. Within a few years he had broken the franchise record for tackles with 224.

'When Pat had entered his restricted free agent year after his third year, he had just set the tackle record,' recalled McGinnis. 'I mean, he was that dude, he was just that dude.'

His performances on the field had turned the heads of their future division rivals. The St Louis Rams head coach, Mike Morris, had set his sights on making the tough-tackling Tillman the centrepiece of his defence's secondary. Morris had welcomed the free agent Tillman to the team's facility for a visit. Pat Tillman's agent, Frank Bauer, went with him and the Rams offered the defender a lucrative contract. By that time Dave McGinnis was Tillman's head coach in Arizona.

'We were paying him $550,000 on his third-year contract,' McGinnis said. That figure was only a fraction of what a top safety could earn at that time. Tillman's salary was reflective of the rookie contract handed to seventh-round picks.

'Well, the Rams offered him over $7 million for three years,' McGinnis recalled. Coach Mack knew that the Cardinals were going to lose their star safety because there was no way that they could match that kind of money. Much to the coach's surprise, the next day he saw Tillman in the locker room, getting ready to hit the gym. 'I said, "Tell me, what are you doing?" and he told me plain and simple that he was getting ready to work out.'

'I said, "Look, your agent called. I know what the offer was. You've earned this. That's the business. God bless you, good luck to you, I am all for you. I always have been and always will be.' McGinnis understood the business of sport, and opportunities for players in Tillman's position to earn $7 million were not handed out like candy. The Cardinals' head coach had resigned himself to losing his defensive asset.

'He said, "What are you talking about, Coach? You and the people here were the only people that believed in me when I came out of college. For me to leave for money, it's not right." So, he stayed,' McGinnis explained.

Through speaking with Dave McGinnis, it is clear that is who Pat Tillman was. He was honest, devoted, extremely hard-working, and humble. On the Pat Tillman Foundation's website there is a section dedicated to Pat's story. The site says that his success never went to his head or broke his principles.

According to the Pat Tillman Trust, the former Arizona Cardinal would drive to games in the same 'beat up' truck he had in college. He had no mobile phone and chose to read voraciously to develop. He would debate and discuss his ideas with eager listeners, family, and friends.

'So that just tells you what Pat Tillman was about,' McGinnis said.

The horrific events of Tuesday, September 11, 2001 sent shock waves around the world and changed the lives of millions of people across the United States and beyond. Week 1 of the new NFL season had concluded the night before as the Denver Broncos beat the New York Giants 31-20 at Mile High Stadium. That season was the last with 31 teams, as the Houston Texans were introduced the following year. It was also the last time a team had a scheduled bye in Week 1. That bye belonged to the Arizona Cardinals.

'We were scheduled to play in Washington [in Week 2],' McGinnis said. 'I can distinctly remember Pat sitting down in our public relations office just staring at the television. He was staring intently, just watching it. And the *Arizona Republic*, which is the newspaper in Phoenix, put the American flag on the whole back page of that day's edition. It was the day after the attacks.

'Well, Pat cut it out and pasted it on the window of the defensive team meeting room and said nothing else.'

The NFL postponed its Week 2 schedule and resumed the following weekend. Tillman started all 12 of the games he featured in, registering 72 tackles and 22 assists. The 2001 season ended, as too did Tillman's rookie contract with the Cardinals. Having turned down the $7 million offer from the Rams the previous offseason, Tillman was about to become a free agent. He was also set to marry his wife, Marie. The young star had a very important period of his life ahead of him.

As the team parted for the offseason, Pat Tillman told his coach not to worry about him, he was going to get married and report back. By the time the offseason activities began, there was no sign of Tillman. It was as the exercises were wrapping up that the newlywed returned from honeymoon and called his coach. 'He said, "Coach Mack, I need to come see you,"' said McGinnis.

The coach had no idea that Pat Tillman was about to share the life-changing news with him. Coach Mack believed he would be coming into the Cardinals facility to discuss his contract.

'When you are a head coach in the National Football League you have a big desk and people sit on the other side of it when they come into your office to see you,' Dave McGinnis described. 'Not Pat, he pulled up a chair like you and I are talking right now, sat next me, looked me in the eyes and said, "Coach Mack, my brother, Kevin, and I have enlisted in the Army. And I just want you to know that."'.

Tillman had set his mind on getting into the Army via Ranger School. The US Army Ranger School prepares Army volunteers, both officers and enlisted soldiers, in combat arms-related skills. Pat and Kevin Tillman planned to pass the school as Rangers and fight for their country. He told his head coach that it was his time and his duty to serve.

'Knowing Pat like I did, and like I still do, he never did anything on a whim. He never did,' Dave McGinnis explained.

'He was … he was a brilliant man.'

McGinnis did ask him whether he had thought about the repercussions of his decision because it was about to become a major news story. His coach, however, had his back and wanted to make sure that he was ready for all the attention he was going to receive. Tillman simply told him that he was not going to say anything and left that to Coach Mack because that was what his head coach was good at.

'He went to basic training, made Ranger School, and was the standard-bearer for his platoon.' Pat and Kevin Tillman committed to a three-year term in 2002 and were assigned to the second battalion of the 75th Ranger Regiment in Fort Lewis, Washington. The two brothers served in Iraq during Operation Iraqi Freedom in 2003.

Dave McGinnis did not hear from Tillman until they were due to play on the road against the Seattle Seahawks on December 21, 2003. McGinnis described the conversation, 'I get a call and he said, "Coach, it's Tilly." He told me he was back at Fort Lewis with his brother, Kevin. He had been over in Baghdad and, as he was in the Seattle area, he wanted to buy some tickets.' Dave McGinnis was adamant that Pat Tillman was not going to buy tickets to see the Arizona Cardinals play.

Following a conversation with the team owner, Bill Bidwell, Tillman and his party were accommodated in his owner's suite. Although Pat Tillman was insistent on paying, the club would not take his money. He may have been humble but he was already a legend to the organisation.

McGinnis had a suite at the team hotel and hosted the Tillman brothers and their friends the night before the game. Food was laid out for them, and the former safety reconnected with his coach.

McGinnis opened his invitation for Tillman to join him in the locker room the next day to speak to the team. 'He told me that it was not about him, it was about the team, and he just wanted to watch them play,' said the coach. Instead, it was arranged for Tillman to enter the locker room after the game to reunite with some of his former team-mates and meet the new faces who had joined since he signed up for the Army.

'As he was leaving the hotel, he grabbed a handful of cookies and asked me what time I got up in the morning,' remembered McGinnis. 'I said early and then he told me that he wanted to meet up. We met in a Starbucks across the street, which was not surprising as we were in Seattle, and I took Larry Moore, who was my defensive coordinator, with me and we all talked.' This meeting took place on the morning of the Cardinals' game against the Seahawks.

'I asked him what he wanted to do. He told me that he planned to finish out his tour that he signed up for because he felt it was right to see out his obligation. But then he said that he wanted to return to the Cardinals and play again.'

The meeting with his coach was so early that Sunday morning, the team had not met for breakfast. McGinnis invited his former safety over to join them for the meal. Tillman was reluctant to do so because he did not want to distract the players while they were preparing for their big division game. However, Dave McGinnis convinced him, and he crossed the street to the hotel, 'Just to say hello. During Sunday morning breakfast you get ready to play and guys are in there getting ready for the game, but they're also getting their food,' explained McGinnis. 'And I tell you when Pat Tillman walked in the room, I mean, it went from a low murmur to dead silence.

'After the game, I had our PR director Paul Jensen close the locker room. Then I invited Pat and his brother Kevin in.'

McGinnis said that Kevin Tillman felt awkward about being in the locker room and asked to be excused because it was not for him. He told Coach Mack that it was Pat's time, not his. 'So, Pat came in and said his goodbyes then said, "Coach, I'm going to hold you to what you said." And I said, "Well, you absolutely can."'

The last exchange that Dave McGinnis and Pat Tillman had was in that locker room in Seattle. The Seahawks had beaten the Cardinals 28-10, but in that moment the result did not matter. Tillman, who was more like family to McGinnis, was back from war and he was safe. The two had rekindled their bond and hopes were high for what could come when Pat Tillman returned to the roster. Promises had been made and both were happy. It was days before Christmas and both parties felt a renewed vigour from their rendezvous.

Their parting words are heartbreaking, 'He said, "I love you, Coach." I said, "I love you, Pat."'

Pat Tillman and Dave McGinnis would never speak to each other again.

Following their 4-12 season, the Cardinals fired Dave McGinnis at the end of the 2003 campaign. Coach Mack received a job as defensive coordinator for Jeff Fisher's St Louis Rams.

In the build-up to the 2004 NFL draft, the Rams' PR director, Robbie Bourne, called Fisher and McGinnis from the team's draft room. 'I thought, what's going on?' said McGinnis. 'That's when they told me that Pat Tillman had been killed in Afghanistan.'

McGinnis paused as he remembered the accounts of that tragic day. He spoke about Pat Tillman with pride and love. Nearly 20 years since Tillman's death, the pain is still visible.

Pat Tillman was killed in the line of duty on April 22, 2004. He was 27.

The circumstances surrounding his death were deceiving at first. The United States Army initially claimed that he was killed during a firefight with enemy combatants. However, investigations found that Tillman had lost his life to friendly fire.

In the lead-up to the tenth anniversary of Tillman's death, ESPN produced a special feature for its *Outside the Lines* programme, recounting the tragic circumstances around his killing.

'After an Army Humvee broke down in the mountains, Tillman's platoon was ordered divided by superiors so that the Humvee could be removed; a local truck driver was hired as the hauler,' the story read on the ESPN website. 'But the two groups struggled to communicate with each other as they traversed the steep terrain. And the second group soon became caught in a deafening ambush, receiving fire as it maneuvered down a narrow, rocky canyon trail.

'Tillman's group, which had travelled ahead, scaled a ridgeline to provide assistance to fellow Rangers under attack. But a squad leader, Sgt. Greg Baker, misidentified an allied Afghan soldier positioned next to Tillman as the enemy and opened fire, killing the Afghan.' The soldiers were then prompted to begin shooting at what they described as shadowy images. They later learned that those images were Pat Tillman and a 19-year-old boy called Bryan O'Neal.

'I have had a long coaching career in this league and coached for 31 years,' Dave McGinnis said. 'I have been in the league 38 straight years, been around and coached eight Hall of Famers. But there is no player that has ever had the same impact on my life as Pat.

'He commanded the room. He was magnetic. Pat had no limits, and no boundaries. And he would captivate a room as soon as he walked in. Pat was brilliant. And when I say brilliant, I mean brilliant. Both in books and in people, he attracted people to him.'

When we had training camp up in Flagstaff [Arizona], we had three fields, and we were on the upper field. I would always put Pat in the golf cart at the end of the practice because the crowd up there was mobbing him every time he walked down. He had attracted anything from the young kids to the middle-aged to the grandmothers, to the bikers, I mean, he was just a people magnet.

'On the football field, he was just fearless. As a coach in this league, all you ever asked a guy is to be accountable, and just to give you everything he has. He was a favourite in the locker room. He was fiercely loyal and would defend his team-mates.'

Dave McGinnis was the last head coach that Pat Tillman had in the NFL. Coach Mack told me that Tillman embodied honesty, integrity, and loyalty. 'We would sit and talk about things that were not even football,' McGinnis continued. 'He was a brilliant man. His heart was so big.'

McGinnis and Tillman lived near each other in Phoenix. As one would expect from a coach who has worked in the National Football League and college football for so long, he has a lot of connections. McGinnis said that whenever people would come to visit him, they wanted to meet Pat. 'Every time he would come show up at the house, just to say hello,' McGinnis said.

'There is a reason that he's an icon. Not only in Phoenix, but nationally. I speak all over the country on Pat Tillman, because of what he did.

'He was honest to a fault. I remember early in his career; I called him in and told him that he had hit a rookie wall. I explained that I was changing his position to play nickel and I went through the reasons why. When I asked him if he had anything to say he told me he did not like it, but he trusted me.

'He is one of the most unique human beings I've ever met in my life.'

I asked Coach McGinnis how his team-mates felt about him waiving a lucrative contract offer to risk his life for their country. 'A lot of them just thought it was bad,' he told me. 'But some of them probably could not even fathom the fact that he had given up all that money and that he was going to die. But they all knew Pat. By that I mean he was a locker-room favourite. He was just who he was.'

'I never asked him why he decided to do it because I knew he had reasons, legitimate reasons. And his team-mates were the same way.'

Approaching the 20th anniversary of Pat Tillman's death, his coach will have him in his thoughts, as he always does. 'He will never leave my mind,' said Dave McGinnis.

'It's not only inspirational, when you really think about it, and then when I get up on stage and talk about him and start explaining to an audience the type of person he was, and then some of the things that he said, then it just brings into focus the sacrifice that he made. I never quit thinking about Pat, but especially on those days.'

For his career at Arizona State University, Tillman posted 340 tackles, 2.5 sacks, and three interceptions for 37 yards. He would add three forced fumbles, 15 pass deflections, and three fumble recoveries in 60 career games.

During his career with the Arizona Cardinals he made 245 solo tackles with 2.5 sacks. Tillman had 99 assists along with 2.5 sacks, three forced fumbles, and three interceptions.

Both the Arizona Cardinals (#40) and Arizona State Sun Devils (#42) would retire his number. A plaza outside the Arizona Cardinals' State Farm Stadium features the Pat Tillman Freedom Plaza where a bronze statue honours the local icon.

The PAC-10, now the PAC-12, features the Pat Tillman Defensive Player of the Year Award.

Pat's widow, Marie Tillman, is the chair of the board for the Pat Tillman Foundation. She and Pat met at Leland High School in California between 1990 and 1994. She is remarried to Joseph Shenton. They have two children together, Mac and Francesca. Shenton also has three children, but not with Marie.

SECTION 4

American Football: The Global Game

CHAPTER 23

A Team is Born

'When I saw this mannequin, I thought, wow, well, could we start a team with this kit'?

– Terry Millward, founding member of the Farnham Knights British Amateur American Football League Team

FOUR DECADES after the Tea Bowl and Coffee Bowl games, a brand-new American football team was born on British shores. The NFL was becoming popular in Great Britain during the 1980s, with its high octane plays, globally recognised names and television entertainment. People were beginning to witness athleticism and combat that they had never seen before. There was no Sky Sports at that time and only four television channels existed. American football filled the late-night transmission on Sundays, growing a cult following along the way.

Inspired by the gladiators that donned the uniforms, pads and helmets on their television sets, British enthusiasts wanted a taste of the gridiron for themselves. The British Amateur American Football League was formed in the mid-1980s.

As someone who was aware of the foreign sport, Terry Millward had no idea he would become responsible for setting up a British team until one day when he walked along his local high street.

'For me, it kicked off when I was either 12 or 13,' Terry said. 'I had actually watched the NFL at least once a year when the television show *World of Sport* used to have a 30-minute highlight of the Super Bowl in January.' At this time, Terry was working with his friend, Roger Hart. 'It was 1983 or 1984, so I must have been 20 years old,' said Terry. 'This mannequin appeared in the sports shop.'

Farnham is a town in the English county of Surrey, approximately 36 miles south-west of London. Its population is around 40,000, which would have been less in the 1980s. So, to see a mannequin in the window of a corner shop kitted out in an American football uniform on a sleepy Surrey road would have been quite the sight for a twenty-something sports fan.

'I was working with Roger at that time, and he told me he'd seen this mannequin dressed up in an American football kit.'

'The NFL was something different,' Roger Hart said. 'There was an excitement about it and a skill that was something you didn't see in sports in the UK at that time. And when I saw this mannequin, I thought, "Wow, well, could we start a team with this kit … could we start a team?"'

These two Surrey lads had an idea, and they ran with it. But there was just one problem, 'Well, our main issue was we did not have a clue how to play,' Terry confessed.

Clueless, but eager to turn their dreams into reality, they had a strategy. It was a plan so simple; it was blindingly obvious. 'So, the next premise was, well, let's find an American,' Terry declared. 'If someone's American, they must be able to play American football. So where do we find Americans?'

The race was on to find a United States expat living in the area. How hard could it be? 'Well,' said Terry, 'someone we were working with said, "Oh, my next-door neighbour is a serviceman down at Greenham Common."'

Greenham Common is more than 30 miles, and 45 minutes, from Farnham. Until 1992, it was a US Air Force base that had nuclear missiles silos on the premises throughout the Cold War. 'So, we just thought, okay, he is American, he is a serviceman,' added Terry, 'he must know how to play American football.'

Their plan was flawless. All Terry Millward and Roger Hart had to do was meet the American and they would convince him to set up an American football team from scratch and coach a bunch of novices the rules, routes, schemes, and concepts, while holding down a highly important job at one of the most secure military sites in the world.

'We arranged a time when we knew he'd be at home,' Terry recalled. 'Literally, Roger and I went round and knocked on his door.' What could go wrong? Two young British men knocking at the door of a United States military police officer unannounced?

'Bear in mind, Roger and I are not the tallest people,' added Terry, 'and this American military policeman who opened the door is about 6ft 3in, plus an extra eight to ten inches because of the doorstep.'

Marc Salazar served as a security police supervisor at Greenham Common air base from 1983 to 1988. As a security escort, he met a number of high-profile people, including Britain's prime minister for that period, Margaret Thatcher. Speaking in an interview with the *Los Angeles Times*, published January 11, 1989, Salazar said, 'She was unbelievable, she took the air out of the room. They did not call her the Iron Lady for nothing.'

Therefore, picture Salazar's reaction when two diminutive young men appeared at his house. 'We just knocked on his door,' Terry Millward said. 'He opened and he just looked down with an expression that said, "Who the hell are these two?"'

'I was a little surprised when I found two gentlemen stood at my door,' Marc Salazar told me. 'They were pretty major in stature. Roger, I want to say, was of all 5ft 4in.

'And Terry,' added Marc, 'well, he was a whopping five one. I'm around 6ft 3in, so it was kind of a big contrast. I stood there at the door with these two guys, and thought, "Well, I can't just turn them away, let's be polite and hear what they have to say."'

As the saying goes, 'If you don't ask, you don't get,' and so Roger and Terry stepped into Marc's house and spent the next two hours that evening talking about American football, a sport they'd never played but wanted to get involved in.

'He politely listened to us, and we kicked around the idea of starting a team with him,' remembered Roger.

'And from that Marc originally committed to give us around four to six weeks of his time to come all the way to Farnham and whip us into shape,' said Terry.

What began as a few weeks turned into about five years. It certainly was not the time scale that Marc was expecting. 'Yeah, I told them that I was happy to help,' said Marc. 'But it was only meant to be that I would help them get started, assist in promoting and advertising the team, give some advice and stuff like that.

'Of course, I was going to help with initial practices as well because these guys didn't have a clue,' continued Salazar. 'They knew nothing about scheduling practices, they didn't even have anywhere to train.'

Quickly, four weeks turned into six. Time was moving fast, and this fledgling team was nowhere near ready. 'I agreed to extend my help and support, but I was clear that I would only be able to do that for about eight weeks because I was moving. Where I was moving to was even further away, so I wasn't going to commute to coach a bunch of British guys in American football in Farnham.'

Practices began, and the striking Salazar quickly moulded his raw rookies into a squad that resembled a respectable American football team. It was not long before he sensed that the roster he had helped build was too much to give up, regardless of the extra travel time and costs incurred by his move away from the area.

'We were not that far into practice when I realised that I didn't want anybody messing with the things that we'd already been working on with the team,' Salazar said. It was Marc's team. He had helped Roger and Terry find the players, and together they had built something special. They could feel it.

'We built the roster; we had guys we thought could play offence and guys that we felt could play defence. Everyone was keen,' said Terry. All they had to do was learn the playbook through Marc's expertise.

They had no idea what formations were used for certain plays. They knew rugby, but nothing about the forward pass, blocking schemes and bubble screens. Second and two, third and long, they were just words that meant nothing compared to the football they knew.

Terry and Roger recruited the first Farnham Knights players by posting adverts in the local newspaper, the *Farnham Herald*. However, some of the people that turned up failed to make an impression on the American coach.

'We had some guys out there who were interested,' Salazar said. 'They thought the main objective of the game was in striking other human beings and, therefore, have a lot of fun hitting people and stuff like that. But they didn't realise there was a skillset to the game.'

The grit was there, as too was the desire. The eager volunteers had the fundamentals needed to compete on an American football field, they just needed to know what it was they had signed up for. 'So, it was a little bit of a tough road initially,' Marc told me, as he reflected on those early days, 'but we had a really solid core of guys who came out initially and really worked hard. There were about 25 guys who got their heads down and stuck it out that first year and we grew.'

'Yeah, we had people that were, let's just say, not the fittest of people,' Terry recalled. 'They could not play "soccer" football or could not play rugby because of their – I'm trying to be polite – their size and stature. But they would come along, and they felt that they could be part of this, and they were part of it.'

With a US Air Force security police supervisor as their mentor, members of the team were given the privilege of entering the base at Greenham Common during the Cold War to watch games. Nuclear missiles were literally a few hundred metres away.

The site today is a nature reserve with a few metres of asphalt remaining where the runway once was. Some buildings remain, including the air traffic control tower, which now has a museum within the observation deck, where visitors can learn about its military past. A copy of Han Solo's Millennium Falcon once stood in the former silos that housed the nuclear warheads, alongside the fields where people are encouraged to be vigilant for rare species of animals, including poisonous adders. The Millennium Falcon was there because the Star Wars movie, *The Force Awakens* was filmed on the site.

In the 1980s, this 693-acre site had shops that sold American goods, including rare candies. Everything inside the compound could only be purchased with US currency. Cars drove on the right-hand side of the road. American flags waved in the wind while men and women in military uniform marched along the sidewalks. It was a mini-USA. There were sports fields and baseball diamonds, all lined with bleachers that presented a setting for a Hollywood movie, or the famous *Friday Night Lights*. It was from those bleachers that the aspiring American football stars of Farnham watched games.

There was fierce competition in the US Air Force European Sports League. It lasted throughout the Cold War from the 1950s through until 1993.

Steve Rains, a former head coach of the Farnham Knights, walked me across the Common land to point out where he and his team-mates once sat and watched the forces personnel do battle on the gridiron. 'So, we'd come in through the main gate,' explained Steve, 'and basically, as you came through the security checks you came on to the site. It was like you were immediately sent out of England into a different country. It became the USA, all the outlets, shops, school, everything you can imagine were there.' He was pointing to a patch of land that is now overgrown with grass and wildflowers.

'But we would be given instructions to drive up to the flight line and then drive down the runway,' said Steve. 'Nobody came with us once we were vouched for, signed in and allowed through the gate. Everything was fine. So, we drove up to the runway, and then drove along the side of the runway, which eventually led down to a car park.'

For Steve Rains, Terry Millward, and Roger Hart, it was like living the American dream. There was no internet at this time, therefore the only taste of American culture they could get was in movies and on television, if it was scheduled. Nothing was on demand, as it is today. There was no instant news, or sports highlights at the tap of a screen. Whereas we can catch up with the latest from across The Pond in a second today, they relied on the editorial judgement of others.

The friends from a small suburban Surrey town travelled to West Berkshire for hot dogs, burgers, fries, and cold beer. 'Good times,' recalled Roger, 'they were good times.'

Steve Rains became animated as he remembered cheering the local servicemen who had battled it out before him on the gridiron. 'We would see the coaches,' he said, 'our coaches, and they were there on the pitch. We had our hot dogs and felt like we were in the USA.'

Marc Salazar insisted on entering the fledgling Knights, which included a milkman, a hairdresser, aircraft engineers, bricklayers, and bank workers, into the top division of the newly formed Budweiser League, Division 1 in 1986 against well-established big city teams. They won five and lost five in the inaugural season. But the following year, the Farnham Knights went unbeaten, winning all ten of their match-ups and the conference title. This was an excellent start for a team that did not even have goalposts to kick through. Marc described the scene best: 'Well, you have seen grass, right? There was grass, the field was sloped, but at least there was grass.'

Their practice facilities were the local park. Trees line the field, and a metal fence runs along its perimeter, separating it from the road and pavement. Marc used the slope of the field to his advantage: 'It depended on what I wanted to do and how much work I wanted to put the team through,' he said.

'If I wanted to do less work, then I would have the guys practise downhill. If I wanted to do more work, I would have them practise uphill. I mean, that was a big difference.'

There was no National Lottery in the United Kingdom at that time: it was introduced ten years later. Lottery funding has provided first-class sports facilities up and down the country. In the mid-1980s, especially with a niche sport like American football, there were no leisure complexes available to facilitate such luxuries.

'We practised in parks,' Salazar said. 'We practised at an old farmhouse for a while, where we had to go out and clear rocks. We also had to turn car lights on and try to figure out where we could draw lines. I think we might have been moving cow manure around and stuff like that. We were doing everything possible to try and create a space that resembled something like a football field.'

'I think it helped build a lot of bridges between the Greenham air force base and the local community,' explained Terry. 'I mean, the image of Greenham that was televised all around the world was of peace protests. But it was actually a very different story.'

'They learned stuff from us,' said Roger Hart. 'They learned about beer. And we learned about football. So yeah, it was great.'

The Farnham Knights have united hundreds, if not thousands, of people in the local community across the decades since Roger and Terry plucked up the courage to knock on the door of a giant US Air Force military police officer. The club has gone through mergers, name changes and multiple home playing fields. Now known as the Rushmoor Knights, they're big enough to have three teams, but remain true to their humble roots.

One of the club's most famous names is Phil Alexander. He started his sports career as a footballer for Reading youth and Norwich City. Alexander enjoyed an amateur career with Wokingham Town and Bracknell Town, before a friend suggested he had a go at kicking in American football. Speaking to Glenn Price from the website *American Football International* on April 12, 2014, Alexander said, 'A friend of mine encouraged me to go along because I could kick the ball quite well. I did alright for the first year.'

Alexander's early success on the gridiron led him to trials for the World League. He was drafted by the London Monarchs as their kicker. He led the league in points kicked during its inaugural season in 1991 and was the first British player to lift the trophy when they won the World Bowl that year.

Phil Alexander had trials for the Chicago Bears and Houston Oilers, but never made it into the NFL. He then pursued other options and began working in sports business. Alexander eventually became the CEO of Premier League club Crystal Palace. He was the longest-serving CEO of any club in the division, and in 2022 Alexander was named Premier League CEO of the Year at the Football Business Awards. He left the club shortly after and is now CEO at Championship club Bristol City.

Marc Salazar left England in 1988 and returned to the States. For the past 27 years he has been a high school teacher and sports coach. In 2021 Marc was appointed athletic director at a school in Porterville, California.

He told me that he looks back on his time in Farnham with fondness. 'They were the beginning of my adulthood, I enjoyed that very much. I miss all of them. Some of those guys have actually emigrated to the United States. So, there are a few guys living in Chicago, Georgia, Florida, and Utah. And so that is kind of neat that they're now adopted Americans, but they're all good guys. I miss them tremendously.

'They were part of my young adult life, and we all grew up together, so, yeah, I look back on those days with a lot of fun.'

This intensely physical sport, with unity at its core, has brought together countless communities around the world. There are thousands of other Farnham Knights stories, with Phil Alexanders breaking out and making names for themselves from a pastime that once was considered worthy of only a cult following. Whether providing respite and bonding among young military personnel far from home or giving misfits the opportunity to prove they *were* good enough to be part of a team, the cauldron of the gridiron continues to captivate sports fans and audiences around the world.

CHAPTER 24

The Growth of American Football

'I just think that everybody understands now that individual games that are put in Europe are going to sell out very quickly'

– Peter King

AMERICAN FOOTBALL has never been so globally popular as it is now. The National Football League had played 36 regular season games in London from 2007 to 2023, with a minimum of two per year guaranteed at the Tottenham Hotspur Stadium through until 2030.

By the end of the 2023 NFL season, three games had been staged in Germany, the first in Munich in 2022 and two in Frankfurt in 2023. Another was guaranteed for Munich in 2024 as part of the league's initial three-year deal with Germany. It was reported that more than three million people requested tickets for the first game in Munich, with 800,000 people in the virtual queue at the peak time of sales.

In 2024 there will be a game played in São Paulo, Brazil. The South American venue was chosen ahead of Madrid, Spain as the host city, though it is understood that the Spanish capital could be awarded a game in 2025. Brazil has been on the NFL's radar for a few years, and the League counts 38 million fans in the country.

Tom Brady played in that first Munich game, in what was his final year in the NFL, and said after the win that it was an experience that he would never forget. Brady admitted that in all his years of playing in the league, and he played for 23 seasons, he had known nothing like it. The memory of 69,000 fans singing John Denver's 'Take Me Home, Country Roads' will be one that sticks with him forever.

In the early 1990s the World League of American Football was established.

'So, the end of Pete Rozelle's tenure as commissioner,' former Frankfurt Galaxy general manager Oliver Luck explained to me when we met in the city ahead of the Miami Dolphins vs. Kansas City Chiefs game in Week 9 of the 2023 season. 'Pete had been there for a good while [1960–1989]. Most observers would agree that Pete was credited with realising how important television could be for the National Football League and the growth of the game. And towards the end of his tenure, there was a bit of a movement to better understand how the National Football League could make itself more attractive, more friendly, more interesting, more exciting to a global audience.'

There was already a large audience in Canada, even though they had their own version of football. The sport was also growing south of the border in Mexico; however, it was predominantly an American sport.

Unlike baseball, basketball, and ice hockey, American football had very little global appeal. There was an audience for it, but it was not generating international revenue like those other US sports.

'So that was the start,' Oliver Luck said. 'The idea initially was a ten-team spring league, called the World League of American Football.'

There were four teams outside of the United States: Montreal, plus three European clubs, London, Frankfurt, and Barcelona.

'The plan was not so much for player development,' said Luck. 'I don't think that was that important in Pete's mind. It was more designed to get people to understand the game, have a rooting interest, start to follow a team. If you live in Stuttgart in the heart of Germany, how do you choose a team in the United States?'

The National Football League had toured on foreign soil for a couple of decades from the mid-1980s. Starting in 1986, the American Bowl featured at least one preseason game that was played in another country each year. There were 40 preseason match-ups that were taken to Australia, Canada, Ireland, Germany, Japan, Spain and the United Kingdom.

'That was really their phase one,' Luck added. 'American football fans would realise, "Oh, there's the San Francisco 49ers, but Joe Montana is only going to be playing a series." And they were spending huge amounts of money on a ticket to watch Montana for ten or twelve plays. It just was not the same.'

The American Bowl was a good PR push for the league. Its poster boys were sent around the world, they posed for photographs, dressed in their uniforms, and showcased the brand. There is a photo of Joe Montana and Dan Marino sat on a yellow taxi inside Crystal Palace stadium, south-east London in 1986, before the 49ers and Miami Dolphins played a preseason game at Wembley on July 31 that summer.

It was a good start for the league, but it was not enough compared to the success other sports were having globally. The commissioner decided it was time for phase two, which was the introduction of the World League.

Oliver Luck was picked by the Houston Oilers in the 1982 draft, which was the same year the Chicago Bears drafted Jim McMahon. Luck had been a team-mate of Archie Manning in his rookie year, and later played as back-up to Warren Moon. In 1986 he retired from professional football and studied law.

'I got involved with the World League in 1990,' he told me.

Luck had connections with Germany – his mother was German. Therefore, in 1990 he received a phone call from New York. It was the league office. 'They said, "We understand you were born in Germany."'

'I was actually born in Cleveland, but my mother's German,' Luck explained. 'They had all the facts wrong, but they knew there was a connection.' And so, Oliver Luck left the United States and set off for Frankfurt as the general manager of the Galaxy. The only catch was that he had no team. 'It may come as no surprise that there was really literally nothing,' he said. 'I mean, I walked off the aeroplane with a cashier's cheque and I went down to Deutsche Bank to open an account.' Luck had no staff, no office, no stadium contract, nothing. 'It was completely virgin territory.'

The World League of American Football (WLAF) was made up of ten teams. There were the US franchises, the New York-New Jersey Knights, Sacramento Surge, Orlando Thunder, San Antonio Riders, Raleigh-Durham Skyhawks, and the Birmingham Fire. There was the Montreal Machine from Canada. And the European teams were the London Monarchs, Barcelona Dragons, and Frankfurt Galaxy.

The WLAF enforced a talent search initiative called Operation Discovery. It was mandatory for each team to field four players from a pool of football (soccer) players, boxers, track and field athletes, rugby players, and any other top athlete who proved they were good enough to play American football. This is how the Farnham Knights' Phil Alexander got involved.

The former NFL coach John Ralston toured 15 countries and three continents looking for local athletes to convince them to become WLAF players. 'The ultimate would be to have a world league made up of international players,' Ralston said in an interview in 1991. 'We looked at soccer players, runners and jumpers, knowing that if they had the talent to do well in other sports, they might be talented enough to play football.'

In reference to the British talent featuring for the London Monarchs, Ralston explained, 'It will take time for them to learn the game, and it will take longer for it to be natural.' The Monarchs' kicker Phil Alexander already had an advantage thanks to Marc Salazar.

These sportsmen, along with the American talent who were either undrafted rookies or veterans looking for a contract, were invited to Orlando, Florida to take part in the combine in February 1991. The WLAF combine was just weeks before the opening game on March 23.

The WLAF held a draft by positions. Salary standards were modest, with quarterbacks getting $25,000 for the season. This was a fraction of the money star quarterbacks in the National Football League were earning in a game. Kickers made $15,000 and everyone else was getting $20,000 per season.

Along with Oliver Luck as general manager of the Frankfurt Galaxy, the league had an impressive cast of front office personnel and ownership. It had support from 26 of the 28 NFL teams (the Chicago Bears and Phoenix Cardinals said no). WLAF president Mike Lynn had left his job as executive president of the Minnesota Vikings to run the brand-new competition. 'We believe the rest of the world is ready for American football,' Lynn said.

Joining Luck and Lynn in the WLAF were Joe Bailey, who had been a vice president of the Dallas Cowboys for 19 years, and the Bears' Super Bowl-winning general manager, Jerry Vainisi.

Team owners were San Antonio's Tom Landry, the legendary Cowboys head coach who won two Super Bowls for the franchise. Landry served as a bomber pilot during the Second World War. He enlisted when he was 19. Landry's brother had been killed earlier in the war while flying a plane across the Atlantic.

Birmingham owner Gavin Maloof was the former owner of the NBA's Houston Rockets, and Raleigh-Durham's George Shinn was the owner of the Charlotte Hornets. Andrew Brandt, who would later become vice president of the Green Bay Packers and draft Aaron Rodgers, was handed the general manager position of the Barcelona Dragons. Brandt was 32 and a player agent at the time.

Eight weeks before the Frankfurt Galaxy's opening game, which was the league's first game, Oliver Luck hired Jack Elway, the father of the Denver Broncos' superstar Hall of Fame quarterback John Elway, as head coach. Jack Elway had been a coach at Stanford, San Jose State and Cal State-Northridge. He had a .650 winning percentage as a head coach and assistant coach. The previous season, Elway senior had worked as a pro scout for the New York Jets.

'Jack put the staff together,' explained Luck. 'They had the much more challenging part, whereas 98 per cent of my time was not so much on football, but essentially on building a local structure. I had to do all of the hiring, from ticket salespeople to sponsorship acquisition people, to dealing with the stadium and putting the whole game together.

'Germans didn't really know much about the game itself. We had to do a lot of educating, and a lot of teaching. But we wanted to do it in a very fun and entertaining manner.'

In the early 1990s the German conception of American football was skewed completely because the only full-game broadcast in their country was the Super Bowl. With the six-hour time difference between central Europe and the east coast, USA, the NFL's showpiece was not kicking off until after midnight.

And because the only live game the German market received was the razzle-dazzle of the Super Bowl, their expectations of an American football game were inflated. They believed each event featured pre-game shows and half-time performances, with fireworks and cheerleaders. This put pressure on Oliver Luck to deliver for his virgin fan base.

'We had to do it because that's what the folks expected,' said Luck. 'They did not just want to see a sterile football game: first down, second down, third down, punt. You see that anywhere. I think that is what set the Frankfurt Galaxy apart from the others within the then World League of American Football.'

With the former New York Giants quarterback, Mike Perez, as his signal caller, Luck and the Frankfurt Galaxy were ready for kick-off on Saturday, March 23, 1991. The Galaxy hosted the London Monarchs at Frankfurt's Waldstadion in front of 23,169 fans.

Doubts began to set in just hours before the WLAF's inaugural game in Germany. The day before the Monarchs–Galaxy contest, only 10,000 tickets had been sold. Football fans in the United States were waking up on the day of kick-off to reports from the Associated Press that league officials were wondering whether they had any chance of success because of low interest.

Juergen Nitsch, a spokesman for the Galaxy, had said that team officials were hopeful of a further 10,000 through walk-up sales. The situation was the same in Barcelona, where a similar number had been sold for the competition's first ever trans-Atlantic game between the Dragons and the New York-New Jersey Knights. Both stadiums got their walk-ups;

19,223 fans turned up for the game in Spain. The Spanish crowd were handed brochures explaining the fundamentals of the sport. That opening-day event would be their lowest attendance of the season, with 40,875 turning up for their next match-up at home in Week 4.

Back in Germany, local newspapers printed explanations of football terms and rules. 'Our sport is a family-type sport,' WLAF president Mike Lynn said to reporters. 'We want to see if there are going to be any women here, any young children. That's important for our success.'

That was exactly the audience that Oliver Luck made his mission to attract in Frankfurt. 'Well, you know, a smart aleck would say American football is all about taking people's property,' said Luck. 'You know, marching down the field, and the Germans are pretty good at that. And they've shown that in the past.

'I would say that the sports landscape in Germany, and across most of Europe in the late 1980s and early 1990s, was very monochromatic. When we started [WLAF], it was soccer, indoor soccer and then more soccer, right?'

When Luck moved to Frankfurt in 1990, West Germany had just won the FIFA World Cup. In 1991, the German women's national team were semi-finalists at the first ever Women's World Cup.

Whereas in the United Kingdom, sports enthusiasts had other competitions to engage them, such as cricket and rugby, and Americans had baseball, basketball, and ice hockey, according to Luck, there were no sporting options for aspiring German fans other than soccer. 'If you were a young German man and 6ft 4in, 260lb, you were not likely to make it as a soccer player,' Luck explained. 'You might be an aficionado. You might support your local club because your father and grandfather supported Eintracht Frankfurt, or whoever.'

As for attracting women and children to the American football games, the Frankfurt Galaxy GM knew the World League could offer a pleasant alternative to what they would have associated with the Bundesliga at that time because there were still serious hooligan problems at local games.

'When I first arrived here,' Luck recalled, 'I went over to the Waldstadion to watch Eintracht Frankfurt take on Bochum. The ultras were there and they were taking over the standing room only sections. It was 98 per cent male, very few females.

'It was not the sort of thing men would do back then. They would not take their dates out to a game on a Saturday night. Most of the men in the crowd were wearing boots, hats, the whole nine yards. It was a somewhat frightening atmosphere.

'And I remember saying to myself, "This can't be all there is. There's got to be a much deeper well of interest."'

Going back millennia, people have enjoyed the collective effervescence that exists inside stadia. Could the party atmosphere of American football unite families and communities in a way that football could not because of hooliganism?

That was the marketing opportunity for the league. Millions of Germans had emigrated to the United States; therefore, they had that connection to the culture. That, along with the confluence of things in Germany at that time, as the Berlin Wall came down, generated opportunities in the country.

It worked for Luck and the Galaxy. American football found the niche in the market and the sport began to grow. 'If you're going to do well and you're in Europe, you have to do well in Germany,' said Oliver. Germany is the economic engine that drives Europe. It's the most populous country in western Europe. Success in Germany is far more beneficial, financially, than in Luxembourg, Denmark, or Portugal. Which is why the National Football League has staged multiple games there and London in the same year.

Speaking ahead of the first ever NFL regular-season game in Frankfurt in November 2023, the Miami Dolphins' special team coordinator, Danny Crossman, recalled the first WLAF game that was played in the city. Crossman was a captain for the London Monarchs in 1991 and 1992 and played defensive back.

'The very first game in World League history was the London Monarchs at the Frankfurt Galaxy,' Crossman proudly mentioned. 'It's been many, many moons, but yeah, I have played a game here in Frankfurt.' He opened his press conference with that comment.

'I think that foot meeting ball, as we get ready to practise here at the Frankfurt soccer stadium, is something they're familiar with. I think that's the common ground that they share. But as you've seen this game grow over the last 30 years here in Europe, obviously they're very knowledgeable, very passionate about what the National Football League is and what football is and I'm sure they're excited.'

The first points scored in the World League of American Football came from the Frankfurt Galaxy, courtesy of a safety. The London Monarchs running back, Judd Garrett, was tackled in the end zone. Although the Monarchs won that contest 24-11, the London franchise only gained a single yard in the first quarter.

'It was very different from what I was accustomed to,' recalled Crossman. 'It was not college football, and it did not have the pageantry of college football. It was not the National Football League. It was a party. There were fireworks and all kinds of stuff going into pregame. Then once the game started, I remember the first two points in World League history, we gave up a safety. We ran a trap from the two-yard line. So, first points in World League history were a safety. Hopefully we don't have one of those [Miami Dolphins vs. Kansas City Chiefs].

'My whole time in Europe playing, especially in the European stadiums, it was fabulous. The fans are just so passionate. The passion you see in rugby and football and everything else, they brought it to American football, and it was very fun.'

The 1991 season ended at Wembley Stadium, as the London Monarchs took on the Barcelona Dragons in the World Bowl. Crossman had three interceptions in the game, including a pick six. The safety was named World Bowl MVP, with the Monarchs clinching the title with a 21-0 victory.

Later that autumn, NFL owners met to discuss the World League. Despite its success in Europe, the league reportedly lost $7 million in its first year. Television ratings were low but shareholders voted to keep the league going. It was agreed that a further $25 million would be invested.

Despite an American team winning the 1992 World Bowl, the NFL decided to suspend the competition. There was no title defence for the Sacramento Surge. The NFL was forced to reevaluate its plans for international growth.

'I think the NFL felt for some time that they wanted to export the game,' reflected Peter King when we met in Frankfurt. 'But I think people who watched the NFL then didn't want to go see what the equivalent of minor league baseball was.'

King added, 'In the United States, minor league baseball is fun and everything, but you get three thousand or four thousand people there, you're not going to get the same crowd as you get at a Major League Baseball game.'

* * *

During its hiatus, the NFL chose to scrap the North American teams and replace them with European franchises. There was a stronger emphasis on giving talent a chance to develop and shine. Ten games against strong opposition that was led by NFL coaches was far better than progressing through offseason activities and camps.

There was also a new broadcaster on the market. Fox Sports launched in 1994 and they agreed to become financial partners, as well as the official broadcasters.

Joining the Barcelona Dragons, Frankfurt Galaxy and London Monarchs were the Amsterdam Admirals, Rhein Fire, and Scottish Claymores. The Fire were based in Dusseldorf, Germany, and the Claymores in Edinburgh, Scotland, but later Glasgow.

Oliver Luck stayed in Germany and became the Rhein Fire's general manager, helping launch them in 1995. Later that year he became WLAF president and moved to London. Two years later, in 1997, the World League of American Football became NFL Europe.

The Sky Sports NFL pundit, Jeff Reinbold, is an American football coach with decades of experience, having coached in college football, the Canadian Football League, and NFL Europe with the Rhein Fire and Amsterdam Admirals. He looks back fondly at his time in Germany and believes the NFL could benefit from another developmental league like it had in Europe at the turn of the century.

'There are more kids that can play in the National Football League than actually do play in the National Football League,' he said.

'If you remember back in the day of NFL Europe, everybody points to [quarterback] Kurt Warner because he went on the win the Super Bowl and have a Hall of Fame career. But Adam Vinatieri will be in the Hall of Fame, probably as one of the only kickers ever to go in. He kicked for 20 years and won four Super Bowls; he would have never had the chance if it hadn't been for NFL Europe.'

Vinatieri played for the Amsterdam Admirals during the 1996 WLAF season as their kicker and punter. He converted all four of his PAT attempts and scored nine out of ten field goal attempts, his longest coming from 43 yards. Following his season in the Netherlands, Vinatieri was picked up by the New England Patriots as an undrafted free agent.

Three of his four Super Bowl titles were with head coach Bill Belichick and quarterback Tom Brady. Vinatieri won his fourth championship with the Indianapolis Colts and Hall of Fame quarterback, Peyton Manning.

'I could go on and on and on with guys that were able to have good careers in the league,' Reinbold said. 'Guys that would never have been given a chance had it not been for NFL Europe.'

In 1995, the Super Bowl-winning head coach, Doug Pederson, played quarterback in Germany with the Rhein Fire. Speaking last season on the Jacksonville Jaguars' annual visit to London, Pederson recalled his time in Europe and shared his observations of the growth of American football in the UK and Germany.

'Yeah, I go back to the days when I played and playing outside of the US was not as important,' Pederson told me. 'The emphasis was not there, but now, the league has taken the initiative, and all 32 clubs have the initiative to play overseas and outside of the US.

'The sport has grown globally, with all the social media outlets and the way the betting market and things like that go around the world, it's become a popular sport. That's one of the things that I really enjoy about coming here [to London], is when you go to the game, you see Jags fans and you're going to see Atlanta Falcons fans [their opponent in London], but you see NFL fans of all the teams.

'I'm going to see a Miami Dolphins jersey, a Pittsburgh Steelers jersey, a New York Giants jersey, and a Dallas Cowboys jersey. I'm going to see NFL fans and that just tells you that our sport is healthy outside of the United States. We continue to grow that through games like this and we get a chance to stay here and play another game here in the city and it just grows in popularity. Our guys should be proud that they're a part of these moments.'

'Every time I see Doug Pederson coaching on the sideline, I go back to 1995 and Doug Pederson is our quarterback with the Rhein Fire,' said Jeff Reinbold. 'Every time I watch Steve Spagnuolo being the defensive coordinator for the Kansas City Chiefs, I think about "Spags" coaching in Barcelona [1992] and later at the Frankfurt Galaxy [1998]. So of course, there is still an awful lot of NFL Europe influence in the National Football League today.'

'It was a huge game-changer for me and many guys that came before me,' the former Rhein Fire defensive back, Nick Ferguson told me. Nick played with the Fire in 1998 before moving to the CFL with the Winnipeg Blue Bombers. Ferguson's biggest success came with the Denver Broncos, where he played for three years. In 2006 he had his best season with the Broncos, pressuring Tom Brady into throwing a 100-yard interception in the AFC Divisional Round playoff against the New England Patriots. The Broncos beat Brady's Patriots in Denver but lost the AFC Championship Game to that season's Super Bowl winners, the Pittsburgh Steelers.

'NFL Europe gave players that opportunity,' Ferguson said. 'It gave guys the reps that are required to develop into a great player in the National Football League. Unfortunately, they had some financial issues. But what it did prove is that the NFL should have somewhat of a spring league because it is a great place for a player to hone his skill set.'

Ahead of the Kansas City Chiefs' first game in Germany in 2023, where they have international marketing rights, quarterback Patrick Mahomes was asked by a German reporter whether time spent in a league such as NFL Europe would have been good for his development. 'I think the playing would have definitely helped,' Mahomes answered.

However, there was a caveat, 'The one thing I think would be just the learning I got from [Chiefs' starting quarterback] Alex Smith and Coach [Andy] Reid. I know it was late in the spring and everything like that. But I remember Coach Kingsbury [Mahomes's college coach at Texas Tech, Kliff Kingsbury, played for the Cologne Centurions in 2006] playing NFL Europe and he had a great experience doing that. Just like my dad playing in minor leagues, playing football against any top competition helps you get better.'

Players got their big break, coaches developed, and Super Bowl champions were nurtured from NFL Europe. Quarterback Kurt Warner was living proof that a superstar could come from it, if given the chance. He was playing arena league football before the Amsterdam Admirals came calling. Following his season in the Netherlands he joined the St Louis Rams and was the main protagonist with the 'Greatest Show on Turf' as they won Super Bowl XXXIV in 1999.

The problem was that the competition was not making any money. Peter King explained, 'As a lot of the teams in Europe are finding now, you can get a foothold, like in Dusseldorf. And in a lot of these places where there are tremendous fan bases, and people love the National Football League.

'But [NFL Europe] was just not going to be the same as if Tom Brady or Patrick Mahomes comes over. For example, in England, the Premier League, you are going to have huge attendances. But as you go down the tables, the crowd numbers become a lot less.'

Jeff Reinbold described a visit his Rhein Fire team made to the London Monarchs at Tottenham Hotspur's former White Hart Lane stadium, 'I can remember pulling into that stadium, when we played in London. For each road game the coaches, players, staff were given two tickets in case we wanted to invite friends or whatever.

'So, I had two tickets. At that time, I did not know anybody in London. So, I got off the team bus and walked across the street. On the other side of the road was a pub. I walked in, and it was like those old wild west movies where the drifter walks in, and everybody looks over their shoulder.

'So, I walk into this pub, and I'm dressed in my coaching gear, and they look at me as if I am some strange outsider. I went to the bartender, and I said, "Hey, listen, here are two tickets for the football game next door." Well, next door was Tottenham's White Hart Lane stadium. They look at me as though they are saying, "Tottenham's not playing today, what are you talking about?" But I could not give two tickets away.'

Oliver Luck's party plan had worked in Germany. Fans flocked in their thousands to games and a genuine rivalry had formed between the Frankfurt Galaxy and Rhein Fire. Speaking to The Athletic, Curt Menefee, the Fox Sports broadcaster who called eight World Bowl games from 2000 until the competition ceased in 2007, said, 'The Deutschland Derby, between Frankfurt and Rhein, was always in the last three weeks of the season, and they had 40,000 people. You may have a game in Barcelona, and Barcelona's a great freakin' place, but there's 6,000 people there. It's the LA of Europe in a way, in that you have beaches and sunshine and, "Yeah, we'll show up at the game later." In Germany, there was 40,000, whether it was at Rhein or Dusseldorf.'

The German market was captivated. In England, interest in the London Monarchs was waning. They failed to win a title after the inaugural World Bowl in 1991. Attendances were dropping. They moved from Wembley to White Hart Lane but struggled to fill that stadium.

In 1998, it was decided that the London Monarchs would become the England Monarchs and the team toured the country in a bid to attract fans. They played in Birmingham, Bristol, and London. However, the plan failed and after the end of that campaign the franchise moved to Germany and became the Berlin Thunder. The Thunder won three titles in four years, including back-to-back World Bowls in 2001 and 2002.

The Barcelona Dragons remained until 2003 and then became the Cologne Centurions. Germany had definitely cornered the market. The only team that lasted the course from the World League of American Football's inception in 1991 was the Frankfurt Galaxy. The Amsterdam Admirals and Rhein Fire continued until the end, but their entry into the league came with the rebrand in 1995.

It is fitting that Oliver Luck's Galaxy had won more World Bowl titles than any other team (four). They kicked off the first ever WLAF game and featured in the final contest, losing 37-28 to the Hamburg Sea Devils on June 23, 2007.

'I think one of the things that has been surprising even to people in the NFL is a scene like you're seeing in Frankfurt,' Peter King told me whilst we were awaiting Patrick Mahomes's arrival at the German national football team's headquarters in the city.

'At least from the media attention, it's probably double what it was in Munich [in 2022], where Tom Brady was involved in the first ever regular-season game in the country. That has been a real surprise. But I just think that everybody understands now that individual games that are put in Europe are going to sell out very quickly. It helps obviously, to have Patrick Mahomes, Tom Brady, and all that. But as the experience in London has shown, anything that has the NFL logo on it is going to do pretty well. So, I've been a little surprised at the mania, and how huge it has been. But I wouldn't say I'm shocked because in the last decade, everything the NFL touches turns to gold.'

* * *

Marc Sessler and the *Around the NFL* podcast have been massively influential in providing news and educating American football fans in Europe. The podcast has strong audience figures in the UK and Germany, with the hosts taking live shows to London annually.

'I think it's kind of like the perfect storm of a number of different things,' Sessler explained when reflecting on the NFL's growth around the world.

'I don't discount the importance of how fantasy football brings all sorts of people into the sport. It can be through a friend group or your family, but you have this fantasy football team, and you start to become emotionally invested in your players, so much so that you are tracking their progress each week.

'Think back a few decades ago and you'd listen to the radio for sports reports and the only baseball team you knew about was the New York Yankees. Due to a lack of access, the only team you knew were the Yankees. That was your baseball world. But now fantasy football has brought the entire league to everyone.'

American football fans of a certain age in the United Kingdom and Germany would attribute the growth of the NFL to accessibility. Throughout the 1980s and 1990s, the only way to follow the league was via highlights shows that delivered the action a week later, newspaper scores on a Tuesday, or through a crackly radio transmission on AM sound waves, which may have been interrupted by a taxi signal as a cab went past the house.

'I go back to the highlight shows that were shown in Great Britain in the 1980s,' Peter King said. 'I just think today's growth is down to the exposure of the game.'

A lot of it is the same way as the Premier League is getting a lot more exposure in the United States now. I remember a couple of years ago, there was a game on a Sunday afternoon. It was at one o'clock Eastern time. Manchester United against Manchester City. And I was shocked when I saw the TV ratings, 960,000 people watched it. That was a huge audience for a soccer game competing with the NFL.

'I honestly think that if you looked at the ratings of a big football game, American football, that was shown on TV in Britain versus a Premier League game, you are going to get a lot of people to watch that game because people have fallen in love with the NFL. I believe it is down to exposure to the game, plus a little bit of the pageantry that comes with it. But on top of it, one of the biggest issues that the UK had and beyond, before television and online access became what it is today, you just could not watch these games the same way.'

'I think the ability to consume the NFL is much easier now,' Oliver Luck said. 'Maybe it is a bit more expensive, because there are so many apps and services that you have to subscribe to, to get all these games.

'In Germany and the UK, it literally used to be a magazine show. In Germany we started with Premiere, which had been a broadcaster up in Hamburg, behind the paywall. They were doing a magazine show, I think they just did the Super Bowl live, that was really it, maybe another playoff game live. There is a lot more content that people can access now. It was hard to be an American football fan because you just could not get much content. If you lived in the old American occupation zone, you could put up your coat hanger and get the broadcast from the American Forces Network. And I did that with friends. I know a lot of Germans did that too. You could not get scores until the Tuesday morning in the *International Herald Tribune*. This was not that long ago, back in the 1980s, even in the early 90s.'

Luck explained to me how he would follow his Houston Oilers but could not find out if they had won until midweek. Phone calls were very expensive during peak hours, and international calls would cost hundreds just for a few minutes.

Now the consumption of content is instantaneous. No matter where fans are in the world, they can access big plays as they happen. As Oliver Luck explained, with the right subscription, NFL fans can watch any game, anywhere at any time. If they want to hear about their team, there are reporters presenting podcasts on demand. Reports in the *LA Times* can be as instantly accessible in Thailand as they are in California.

'I think the fans are much better educated now than they were back in that era,' Luck summarised. 'And, you know, the world has gotten smaller. Therefore, people travel to the US for an NFL game. There was not a lot of that happening back in the 1990s. So, it's all opened, thanks mainly to technology.'

Social media has allowed fans to come together, forming communities where people with shared interests can moan, cheer and rant about their teams. 'If your team goes through a dark period,' said Marc Sessler, 'you can jump out and care or not care because there are a million other things to do.

'But I don't know how you can really be a casual NFL fan in Europe, because you have already made the choice to hang out with this gang of people that are watching these games in the middle of the night. The schedule is completely different to anything relating to normal.'

As Marc highlighted, these social communities provide a platform for people to connect with like-minded folk from the comfort of their own living room. While loved ones sleep upstairs, fans can celebrate in silence with friends that they have never met. The online communities continue to grow because the fans who are in them are completely invested. The roots of their fandom stem from a collective that is equally devoted and obsessed.

Speaking about the collective, Marc Sessler said, 'The one thing that always blew me away when my co-hosts and I first travelled to England with the *Around the NFL* podcast was that we would meet up at a random pub and hundreds of people turned up to say Hi.

'It was genuinely great to talk to them all because they did not talk so much about football but chatted to us about the conversations we had been having on the show. But you could tell they were really passionate and knew a lot about American football. I mean, it was higher than the average American fan.'

It was the community that impressed Marc most. Strangers that had come together through American football, many of whom had decided to meet face-to-face for the first time at NFL London events.

These online communities are places where fans can form fantasy football leagues, share insights, information, highlights, and instant access. The NFL games in Frankfurt and Munich took fans on every continent inside Deutsche Bank Park and Allianz Arena, venues that, 30 years ago, were viewed as concrete pantheons from a mystical land. Though they were different stadiums in the 1990s.

Stadiums have changed; so too have sporting experiences. The Premier League, Bundesliga, NFL, and MLB all learn from one another. Oliver Luck's vision for sports entertainment in Germany was no fluke. Although when he landed in Frankfurt with his banker's cheque, the thought of the reigning Super Bowl champions hosting a home game in the city would have been beyond his wildest dreams.

CHAPTER 25

The Next Step

'The sky is the limit, man. Hopefully in the future, we see something crazy like a division over here'

– NFL linebacker, Bradley Chubb

AMERICAN FOOTBALL has had a clear vision over the past couple of decades. Expansion. Ever since former commissioner Pete Rozelle launched his campaign for the World League of American Football, the NFL has wanted to boost its coffers through international growth. New markets bring fresh opportunities to sell the product and generate merchandise revenues.

Part of the reason why WLAF and NFL Europe struggled in their markets was because the product was not the same as fans had grown accustomed to. As Peter King pointed out, it was American football, but without the household names and elite talent.

Therefore, the league decided to give the fans what they wanted: proper NFL games.

Just months after NFL Europa contested its last World Bowl in June 2007, the National Football League took a regular season game between the New York Giants and Miami Dolphins, two of its most popular franchises, to Wembley Stadium in London.

NFL commissioner Roger Goodell had taken over from Paul Tagliabue in 2006, and had agreed to make the bold step into a brave new world.

As the two regular season games in Frankfurt wrapped up during mid-November 2023, I spoke to Henry Hodgson, the general manager for NFL UK. Henry had worked for NFL Europe since 2003 and was a member of the team that brought the first international game to London. He worked closely with the former managing director, Alistair Kirkwood, in establishing NFL UK. 'NFL Europe had been around for some time,' Hodgson said.

'Alistair and I worked on what became NFL UK.'

Their task was to provide American football fans in the United Kingdom with a product that filled the void left by the dissolution of the country's two representatives in NFL Europe, the London Monarchs and Scottish Claymores.

What they found was that the UK fan base did not want a weaker competition. NFL Europe had imported star talent that fans in Britain, Germany, the Netherlands, and Spain got to see, but those players were gone after ten games. The talent that remained on the field was not NFL calibre, and in a country that has so many top-tier competitions, people needed to be wowed.

'So, if you are going to be successful in exporting American football and the NFL, you have got to do it with the best product,' Hodgson explained. 'If you were Pepsi, you wouldn't say "Let's create a different product that's not quite as tasty as Pepsi is for the UK." And likewise, there was no way we were going to do the same with the NFL.'

And with that, NFL UK was born. It was a roll of the dice, but Henry, Alistair Kirkwood and the team felt confident that they could pitch the idea of playing a regular season game in London to the National Football League.

In 2005 the NFL hosted its first ever regular season game outside of the United States. The Arizona Cardinals were the home team and took on their division rivals, the San Francisco 49ers, at the Azteca Stadium in Mexico City. It was a huge success with 103,000 fans in attendance. The Cardinals won 31-14.

Henry Hodgson revealed that NFL UK had bid for that international game. 'That was really the trigger point,' Hodgson said. 'We didn't get that one, and we knew it was understandable. We pitched for it at short notice. And, of course, Mexico City is literally closer.'

The NFL UK office had the bit between their teeth and were determined to make the National Football League an offer they could not refuse. 'What would a really great offer look like for us to do that going forward?' said Henry.

Alistair Kirkwood took his presentation to Roger Goodell, who was the NFL's chief operating officer at that time and it was compelling enough to the future commissioner that the league agreed to send a game to London.

'We did not have an awful lot of time from it being greenlit to then getting the game on track for the following October [28, 2007],' Hodgson explained. 'We didn't really know what we were going into. I remember when we first announced it and invited fans to register their interest for tickets during Super Bowl week.'

People clicked on a link and put in their details. Throughout the first 16 hours Henry repeatedly hit refresh on his browser and watched the number tally at a rate that was beyond his expectations. 'We had 500,000 individual applications in a very short space of time through the first day or so.'

NFL UK's pipe dream had become a reality. Alistair Kirkwood's pitch and presentation to Roger Goodell had been vindicated. NFL in London was suddenly viable.

'And then it became about not only making the game happen, but also everything around the events, such as the fan engagements during the week, and all of the experiences that help the UK fan base to grow.'

It was their opportunity to show that games in London could be a permanent fixture on the NFL calendar. At that time, Hodgson, Kirkwood, and the UK team were unaware whether the New York Giants vs. Miami Dolphins at Wembley Stadium would be a one-off event or the first of many.

It was a journey into the great unknown, not only for two storied NFL franchises, but also NFL UK. Roger Goodell played a role, along with others, in establishing which two teams would compete. The Wembley match-up needed to have an appeal for fans, so the Dolphins and Giants made logical sense. They were two franchises that were very popular from the 1980s. American football fans were being given two solid teams, although Miami's 0-7 record heading into London that season was the worst in their history at that point.

The Giants had lost their two opening games but flew over on a hot streak, winning five in a row.

The NFL UK team knew that if they wanted the London games to become a regular event, they had to impress the clubs. The Dolphins and Giants had to leave with a positive feeling. Their experiences were crucial because they were going to be the advocates to 30 other clubs. What London required was for the Dolphins and Giants to tell the others that they needed to give it a go.

'So, we really worked very closely with both clubs, and especially with the Miami Dolphins as the home team, to make sure that what they had in London was a terrific experience,' Hodgson said.

And that is exactly what both teams got. More than 81,000 fans braved the rain and witnessed household names such as Eli Manning, Brandon Jacobs, Michael Strahan, Osi Umenyiora, and defending NFL Defensive Player of the Year, Jason Taylor.

'We developed a 50-foot Jason Taylor robot that roamed around London,' remembered Hodgson. 'It was intended to be a big marketing tactic for us to get the message out about the game. I think when Jason Taylor saw it, he was like, "What the hell is this?"

'But it was intended to bring attention and it probably did that. Albeit it looked a little bit strange.'

The game was not a classic. New York won 13-10, but fans left feeling satisfied. Top-class sport that had been so distant just a decade before was now on their doorstep. More importantly for NFL UK, each team enjoyed their experience.

'We won the game, everybody had a good time here in London and hopefully we'll come back,' New York Giants defensive end Michael Strahan said. 'The atmosphere was phenomenal, better than I anticipated. It was like being at home.'

The Giants' head coach, Tom Coughlin, was equally complimentary. 'Our team was very proud to be here in London,' he said. 'The people have been wonderful to us. The stadium is beautiful.'

Miami's coach, Cam Cameron, left with a positive impression, despite his team suffering its eighth straight defeat, 'I can't imagine a game being put on better than this. The hospitality was like none I've ever seen.'

It was a success for NFL UK, the fans, teams, and the league. The London game provided food for thought for the commissioner and opened up marketing opportunities for the competition.

Oliver Luck had been successful in expanding the sport in Germany with his vision of mixing entertainment and culture, so did he ever envisage a period where the National Football League would take its product on the road during its short season?

'I am not sure we reasonably expected an X-number of NFL games to take place over in Europe,' he said. 'But I distinctly recall that first World Bowl at Wembley Stadium between the London Monarchs and Barcelona Dragons. There were more than 90,000 people there.

'We had a very mediocre team that first year of the Frankfurt Galaxy, which was the spring of 1991. We won seven games but were bottom of our division. By the time of our final game, we were already out of the playoffs.

'We played the Sacramento Surge in Germany and 52,000 people came.' The team had nothing to play for, but people came out in their thousands to be there. 'They had a great time,' Luck added. 'So, it didn't take much to understand that the German crowd really got American football.

'I don't think we had any sort of idea of when all this [NFL regular season games in Europe] would happen. But there was some thought given by the NFL folks for years about "Okay, what's next?"'

Without NFL Europe, there would not have been NFL London games, and later Germany games. The league educated people on the continent and grew developed fan bases where they perhaps would never have existed.

Lessons were learned from a logistical standpoint as well, which no doubt would have helped build the confidence in Roger Goodell when he ultimately decided to take an asset overseas, that asset being the millions of dollars a single NFL game generates.

'I would say because quite a few of the people involved with NFL UK had been involved in NFL Europe, I suppose when it came to the logistics of flying the stuff that the teams needed, how to get equipment over to the UK, there was a lot of expertise,' said Henry Hodgson. 'Literally in freight cargo, flying stuff around, so it wasn't like we were coming at it trying to figure all those things out.'

Hodgson takes a lot of pride from his time working with NFL Europe. The experience gained has taken him to Los Angeles en route to becoming the general manager of NFL UK. He has helped oversee the incredible success of international games in Great Britain, from those early games to the expansion of multiple games at multiple venues within such a short timescale.

When comparing the success of the NFL London games in relation to the NFL Europe era, Henry said, 'I think, from an NFL Europe standpoint, the difficult thing was that probably it was pretty clear that 80 per cent of the rosters were not good enough to play in the National Football League. And the 20 per cent who were came to Europe and then never came back again. So, you had to resell the ones that were good enough if they stuck around.'

As good as it was to have the likes of Kurt Warner, Dante Hall and Brad Johnson establishing their names in Europe, they went back to the States and forged their careers. The best talent that NFL Europe had to offer disappeared in the blink of an eye. Fans could claim them as their own, but ultimately, they were like the loan stars aiding a second-tier football team into the Premier League or Bundesliga. As soon as their talent had been recognised, they were called back and competing for major honours.

Therefore, from a marketing and public relations standpoint, it was challenging for NFL Europe to sell a brand that had its headline acts continually taken away. What turned out to be the better option was global brands with superstar talent competing at one of the biggest stadiums in the world. Selling the best players of their sport to new fans was much simpler and it satisfied the existing American football fan base.

NFL regular season games were beyond Peter King's wildest dreams. He has become a huge advocate of international games and has experienced the first games in Munich and Frankfurt. He said, 'Until a few years ago, I never thought the NFL would play regular season games [abroad]. Often, I thought they might someday.'

Six years after the Miami Dolphins hosted the New York Giants at Wembley Stadium, the league decided that two games a year could head across The Pond.

For a conservative organisation such as the National Football League, the agreement to send two games to London was monumental and not something they had taken lightly. It was a big leap for the sport. At that time there were not many sports leagues, and none of the major competitions, that sent multiple games overseas. And this was a big leap. More leagues have followed the NFL's lead and hosted regular season games from their respective championships abroad, but even by modern day standards, multiple contests outside of their domestic setups are relatively unheard of.

What made this choice by Roger Goodell even more unique is that the NFL season is very short. In 2013 the NFL regular season was only 16 games. This was extended to 17 in 2021, with one eye on the international schedule. By comparison, the NBA regular season is 82 games, and Major League Baseball is 162 games.

'This is picking up proportionally a significant piece of the season,' explained Hodgson. 'To bring it overseas and to the UK was a big deal for them and for us. So, I think once they saw that not only was it successful, but it also brought a whole new element to the league.'

Added interest from within the United States was generated by the London games. This interest meant more revenue for network partners, who suddenly had more airtime to sell around games that might not have otherwise received as much attention.

'They were also selling out a large stadium in London,' said Henry. Those multiple sellout crowds brought increased marketing, media, and merchandise revenue. 'I think it was a relatively natural next step to go to two, then three, then four games.'

When the NFL opted to play multiple games in London, the Jacksonville Jaguars committed one of their home games to the UK each season. Their billionaire owner Shahid Khan had only purchased the franchise the year before their first venture into London, but he saw the unique possibilities and committed to it.

'I think the Jaguars have been incredibly influential,' explained Henry Hodgson, 'because they have made that move and they have seen the opportunity themselves.'

Speaking at an event in London on the eve of the Jacksonville Jaguars' game with the Buffalo Bills in 2023, which was the first time a team had played consecutive league games internationally, Khan acknowledged that the franchise's relationship with the UK had paid dividends. 'It's a win-win-win,' said Khan. He was explaining how the investment had been a success for London and American football fans in Britain, a success for the Jaguars, and delivered success to the city of Jacksonville.

'We'd love to see it go forward,' Khan added. The Jaguars celebrated ten games at Wembley Stadium in October 2023. Their 23-7 win over the Atlanta Falcons in Week 4 of that season kick-started a five-game winning streak, with all five wins coming at different stadiums.

Khan has tried to make Wembley the team's home from home, and he saw his plan pay off. 'It's moved the needle gradually along,' Khan said.

'Our colours are there [at Wembley]; the energy in the crowd is there. The number one jersey I saw was [Jaguars quarterback] Trevor [Lawrence]. Definitely, it compares favourably with Jacksonville.'

I have been a part of every Jacksonville Jaguars game in London and have spoken to numerous fans who have made the trip from Florida. None have knocked Khan or the franchise for taking one of their precious home games from them. They only get eight a year, nine every other year. The Jaguars fans appreciate the exposure it has given their club. Jacksonville is a small city in northern Florida with a population of less than a million. It is not the biggest market in the National Football League. TIAA Bank Field has a capacity of just under 68,000. The London games give the franchise its own space in a congested schedule. Also, they present the Jags with fresh marketing opportunities and bonus merchandise sales to a sold-out 85,000 crowd.

In 2023, as the Jaguars won in London for the second straight week, beating AFC hopefuls the Buffalo Bills, they made a statement. If Jacksonville are to play consecutive games in London moving forward, few teams are going to want to face them. The Jaguars have a clear advantage. They have mastered the logistics, they know the city, they have a solid fan base, and they have the luxury of it being a true second home. Khan's plan has worked.

'They have made that commitment to play here every year,' said NFL UK's Henry Hodgson. 'So, for us looking at what the next potential outcome may be, could you have a franchise in the UK? And for a team like the Jags to raise their hand and say, "Okay, we'll help you with that experiment by playing on a regular basis," and determining what works, what does not, how you can improve things, and so on. It helps us get into a better situation should the opportunity arise down the road.'

A lot of what NFL UK has done has been to test various strands on an annual basis in order to learn more. Therefore, if that opportunity arises, be it a franchise or European division, as teased by NFL commissioner Roger Goodell during a visit to London, the league is prepared for it.

'And you can say, "Great, we've done this,"' said Hodgson. 'That goes from a team playing annually and then back-to-back in the same season, which the Jags have done. It is all of those learnings that come out of that, plus the early kick-off versus late kick-offs, it's not taking a bye week after your game in London. Fortunately, the Jags had a great run, both in London and then after London [in 2023]. So, the Jags have been, I think, an important partner in that they were the ones that made that commitment and have done for ten years, but also that they have been willing to say, "Alright, what's the next evolution? What can we help you with now?" It's not massive learnings in one go. But you pile up those learnings over time. And it is incredibly important.'

Arsenal's owner, Stan Kroenke, committed to sending his Rams team to London for a run of seasons while the franchise moved from St Louis to Los Angeles and had SoFi Stadium developed.

Whether it was the first game in 2007 or the next in London or Germany, it is vital for the league that teams have a positive experience. That was the goal when the league made the bold step across the Atlantic Ocean, and it worked.

Germany provided an additional logistical challenge in that it is another hour ahead. However, Munich received the biggest endorsement it could have had in 2022 when the greatest quarterback to play the game, seven-time Super Bowl champion Tom Brady, announced at the end of his visit, 'That was one of the great football experiences I've ever had. So that says a lot for 23 years in the league, and for a regular-season game, I think the fan turnout was incredible. It felt very electric from the time we took the field. At the end of the game with them singing "Sweet Caroline" and "Country Roads", that was pretty epic. I think everyone who was a part of that experience got to have a pretty amazing memory for their life. Thank you for hosting us. We appreciate it. Thank you.'

Brady's Tampa Bay Buccaneers had just beaten the Seattle Seahawks 21-16 at Bayern Munich's Allianz Arena on November 13, 2022. Speaking at the post-game news conference, he added: 'I've played at Wembley twice. I played in Estadio Azteca in Mexico, which was another amazing experience, and this is as good as it gets. To just travel around the world and see kind of the welcoming from even around town, there was a lot of really cool fanfare, and then driving in today it looked like there was a lot of excitement. By the time we got on the field for warm-ups, the stadium was basically full, and it just gets everyone hyped up, and hopefully we kind of entertained everyone. That was our goal coming out here.'

The Baltimore Ravens head coach, John Harbaugh, has been the biggest name to openly criticise the international games. After the Ravens lost 44-7 to the Jacksonville Jaguars at Wembley in 2017, Harbaugh declared, 'I do not plan on going over there any time soon to play again. Somebody else can have that job.'

His Ravens team found themselves 37-0 down in that game. Harbaugh explained how culminating factors led to an overall negative experience. 'There were certain things that came up that you looked at and go, "That wasn't ideal,"' he said. 'We have no control over where to stay, how far the bus ride is and how long it takes us to get to the stadium and those kinds of things.'

Six years later, his team was back in the United Kingdom. Instead of flying in on the Friday to play on Sunday, they spent the week in London to acclimatise. The Ravens reaped the rewards with a 24-16 win over the Tennessee Titans. After the victory, Harbaugh sang a different tune: 'It's a great feeling,' he said. 'Better than the alternative by far. I can tell you that. A great experience. It's a lot better when you win, I can tell you from experience. Glad to be here. The fans are great. The fans were loud. I love the singing. It was a loud stadium. It was like a home game, like an NFL game as far as the fans. I thought they were very knowledgeable. They know the game over here. That was impressive to see. Just a very impressive crowd.'

The greatest ambassadors for the international games are the players and coaches, as Hodgson had explained about needing the Giants and Dolphins players to have a great experience in that first ever London game. And in Frankfurt, 33 years after Oliver Luck had arrived with no team, no staff, just a banker's cheque and a vision, NFL stars were clearly buoyed to be there.

'I think it's fabulous,' the Miami Dolphins' special teams coordinator Danny Crossman told me when I asked him how he felt about being back after having been involved in the first ever World League of American Football game decades earlier.

'It's well-earned by these other countries that the NFL is reaching out to and traveling to and hopefully there's more to come. From what we understand, there will be more to come. I think it's just going to be a continual process of spreading this game throughout the world. Fans when they see it in person, and that's what you see, there's going to be some guys and girls at the game this weekend that are going to find a player that they think is the greatest thing and follow them for who knows, the next five, ten years and hopefully the Dolphins become somebody's favourite team after this weekend.'

The Dolphins' offensive coordinator, Frank Smith, has German ancestry and was proud to represent his family. 'It's been great,' Smith said. 'Unfortunately, we haven't had much time outside of the hotel, but my great-grandma was born here. She moved to America from Stuttgart so my first trip internationally with my dad was to Germany to Dusseldorf. So, it's awesome.'

Smith added, 'I think when the schedule got announced, I think my dad bought tickets – or I shouldn't say he bought tickets, he requested me to get him tickets to the game probably immediately. I just think it's great. I've been travelling to Germany since I was 11 or 12, and my dad has done business over here for the last 20 years or probably more than that, but I think it's great. It's a fantastic country. Everyone loves sports. American football has obviously been a sport that everyone's enjoyed. To be a part of the first game, for me, I couldn't be happier for us to play here.'

Smith's running back on the 2023 Miami Dolphins offence was Raheem Mostert. Mostert mentioned that his mother is German and, like his coach, he took huge pride in representing his family in the country. 'First off, I love it,' Mostert said. 'It's been welcoming. And yes, I have played in London my rookie year [2015] when I was in my first stint as a Dolphin. It's a lot of fun. Truthfully, my family is from here. My mother was born here about an hour and a half away [from Frankfurt] in Bad Hersfeld – I believe that's right. So yeah, it feels good to be here."

I asked Mostert how important it was for him to play in Germany, given his family ties. 'Yeah, it's fairly important,' he said. 'I would love to tap into my roots a little bit more, just being who I am as a person, as an individual. I love learning about my ancestry and the history behind the reason why I am who I am and also what my family was like back in the day. It's fairly important.'

'I love the fact that the NFL is definitely taking that initiative to go abroad and have these opportunities for players to get outside the norm, being outside the US. I think that's very important to see different cultures and pick up a few things. I know when we first arrived here, Jaylen Waddle was talking about all these different things. Talking about currency and he went to exchange right before we departed and he was fully invested in learning the culture and history behind Germany and stuff like that, which I thought was fairly neat.'

* * *

Following the success of the two Frankfurt games in 2023, which had been preceded by three consecutive games in London, Roger Goodell confirmed that a new international market would be used the next season. A few weeks after the league left Germany, Goodell revealed that 2024 will see the first ever regular-season game played in South America.

London's deal with the NFL runs until 2030, with two games a season guaranteed at the Tottenham Hotspur Stadium. The Jaguars' operations in the UK are separate to the NFL's deal, therefore whatever Jacksonville decide to do will be an addition to the league's scheduled match-ups.

The NFL reportedly invested £10 million ($12.8 million) in the Tottenham Hotspur Stadium's development. League officials regularly visited the site, keeping abreast of construction, with specific American football designs and logistics in mind. Two games have been played at the venue each season since 2019, except the Covid year in 2020. The Jacksonville Jaguars have played there as the home team and road team, winning both games with Trevor Lawrence as their quarterback.

In 2023 the stadium was granted the status as the 'Home of the NFL' in the United Kingdom. In a statement, Roger

Goodell said, 'We are excited to extend our partnership with Tottenham Hotspur through the 2029/2030 season and look forward to hosting future NFL games in the world-class Tottenham Hotspur Stadium, as the Official Home of the NFL in the UK.'

The statement continued: 'Growing the game globally is a major strategic priority for the League. Our commitment to Tottenham Hotspur Stadium will allow us to continue to bring extraordinary NFL experiences to fans in London, while creating a positive social and economic impact on the local community.'

As part of the joint statement, the Tottenham Hotspur FC chairman, Daniel Levy, said, 'NFL gamedays at our stadium are special occasions where we see fans from around the world descend on Tottenham, bringing so much vibrancy to the High Road and supporting our local economy. As the NFL continues to grow its fan base throughout Europe, we are extremely proud to be given official status as the Home of the NFL in the UK and look forward to seeing the excitement that gamedays bring to Tottenham for many more years to come.'

The London mayor, Sadiq Khan, said the economic boost of having two games a year in the city is more than £300 million ($375 million).

With new markets on the horizon, along with games in London and Munich, how far can the National Football League go? Demand is higher than it has ever been, generating millions of dollars for the league. Each time new things have been tested, the results have exceeded expectation.

Speaking in Frankfurt, the Miami Dolphins' star linebacker Bradley Chubb said, 'The sky is the limit, man.' Chubb had played at Wembley Stadium 12 months earlier with the Denver Broncos and spoke from experience regarding international travel. 'Hopefully in the future,' he added, 'we see something crazy like a division over here every year to be able to play in front of these great fans.'

Speaking after the Kansas City Chiefs' 21-14 win over the Dolphins in that Frankfurt match-up, Chiefs quarterback Patrick Mahomes said, 'I'm up for everything,' when asked if he would like to play in Spain. 'I'm excited to get across the world, play football, show American football and what it's done for not only me but for a lot of people across the rest of the world. I thought it was really cool to be out here. The whole experience, being out in the city, the practice facility, you could tell everybody was excited. Like I said, I want to come back. I don't know what this will be, but when I get the opportunity, I hope [Chiefs chairman] Clark [Hunt] jumps at it and we can be back out here playing football games.'

Many of the players that I have spoken to in London, Frankfurt, Munich, Pittsburgh, Phoenix, speak highly of the international experience. There will be some that do not like the travel and the impact it has on their bodies, but overall, the outlook is positive.

Peter King said, 'Now there are five [international games], there is no doubt in my mind that I think the league is not necessarily leaning on a team or teams over here in Europe. I think they're leaning toward more and more events. Therefore, instead of five games in a year, maybe there will be eight international match-ups in five, six, seven years from now.' He was right because at least eight games will be played abroad from 2025.

Nothing surprises him about the league any more. King has been around the game long enough to know that it is an ever-evolving beast. He said, 'especially when you see what happens when the NFL starts to branch out like a few years ago, nobody thought that they would ever have the draft anywhere other than New York City. Then they put the draft in Nashville and it's Friday night with picks being announced in rounds two and three, and there are 600,000 in this one street downtown.

'The NFL has decided to spread the draft around. I think they want to spread international games around as well. I doubt sincerely that they're going to regret it. And the fact now that you have the extra games, due to the 17-week season, those extra games give the league more inventory to play with to put games over here in Europe.'

Oliver Luck, the man who was general manager of the German startups and headed NFL Europe, believes anything is possible. 'When Roger Goodell first got started as commissioner,' he said, 'he wanted to make a $25 billion-a-year revenue league. I'm not sure exactly where they are, but they have really amped it up.

'I don't know the economics, but certainly the television broadcasting rights outside of the United States are worth more than anybody ever expected them to be. I think the percentage of revenue for the NFL coming from international games is still relatively modest. So, there is still a lot of runway left.'

Sitting in the Kansas City Chiefs' hotel in Frankfurt the Saturday morning before the Dolphins and Chiefs game in 2023, Luck spoke with authority about the fan bases in Europe. He has watched the sport grow for three decades and still travels over from the United States. He believes that the league can sell out any game, regardless of the calibre of team, citing the Carolina Panthers and Arizona Cardinals, who were two struggling teams at that point in 2023, but would generate as much interest as the heavyweight AFC clash between the Dolphins and Chiefs.

'You could sell out a stadium in virtually every major European city, as well as Mexico City, Guadalajara and Monterrey, probably throughout Canada. You could even take it to Australia, Tokyo, and I think we would sell out without really much of a problem. But I think it really depends on what they ultimately want to get out of it. Do they want to look like the NBA, which has incredible international players? Those are big questions. So, I'm not sure what the answer is. Although I think it's a wide-open runway. It's interesting.'

Henry Hodgson believes the next step for the league is to explore new markets. It seems natural that for the growth to continue, the NFL branches out into other cities and territories. 'Do we continue growth in Europe?' said Hodgson. 'Are there other markets to look at there? And I think Spain and France are the two obvious European markets that we are investigating to see if we could find the right stadiums and the right cities to partner with to host games in. But then, what about outside of Europe? What would that look like in other markets? And there are lots of other markets that I think would love to host NFL games, be that Australia, or Canada, wherever.'

American football is not a global powerhouse like football and basketball. The sport has a long way to go to establish itself like those, in terms of worldwide competition.

Player development will be important in generating local interest in countries outside of the United States. In the UK the league launched the NFL Academy, which opened in September 2019. The Academy is a major initiative which aims to use American football to create life-changing opportunities for young people all around the world. It offers talented student athletes aged 16–19 a pathway to combine their full-time education alongside a transformative life skills programme and intensive training in the sport, under the guidance of a professional coaching team.

Based at Loughborough's world-renowned centre of sporting excellence, and in partnership with Loughborough College and Loughborough University, the programme promotes world-class performance and the development of elite player pathways, supporting student athletes with NFL best practices and resources.

During the 2023–24 academic year, the NFL Academy supported 61 student athletes from 13 different countries. Nine former NFL Academy alumni played Division 1 NCAA college football in 2023 at top schools including Tennessee, Temple, Colorado, Vanderbilt, Bryant, Mississippi State and Hawaii.

In 2028, the Los Angeles Olympics will see the introduction of flag football as an official event. Flag football is a short, fast, non-contact and gender-equal format, renowned as the most accessible and inclusive version of American football.

It is spearheading exceptional worldwide participation growth in American football, especially among women and girls. An estimated 20 million people in more than 100 countries currently play it, which is growing in tandem with the exploding international popularity of the NFL, as America's favourite spectator sport continues to build on a global fanbase of 340 million.

In 2023, 65 national representative teams participated in the International Federation of American Football [IFAF] continental flag football competition, building towards the biggest-ever IFAF World Flag Football Championships to be held in Lahti, Finland in August 2024.

Any country that makes a run at the Los Angeles Olympics will undoubtedly see a massive take-up in their home markets. For the country that advances to the medal games, the seeds of the sport will be sown, the roots of which could become the foundation of participation and globalisation that is beyond the NFL's expectations.

This non-contact version of the game will engage new fans, unite communities, and nurture the next generation of American football followers, therefore exceeding the current global numbers whose only gameday viewing is in February for the Super Bowl in many of those places.

It is fitting that the Olympic Games will become influential in the development and growth of American football.

The Games are a symbol of peace, whose origins date back millennia with the signing of the Olympic Truce, or *Ekecheiria,* in the ninth century BC between three kings in ancient Greece – Iphitos of Elis, Cleosthenes of Pisa and Lycurgus of Sparta – to allow the safe participation of the ancient Olympic Games for all athletes and spectators from those Greek city-states, which were otherwise almost constantly engaged in conflict with one another.

The modern Olympics continue, to promote that message of peace, which the brave men who found solace on the gridiron for the Tea Bowl and Coffee Bowl games had fought for.

They all risked their lives for our future. Some made the ultimate sacrifice to allow the world to sit together in harmony and enjoy the best of human interactions. Whether that is linking arm-in-arm inside a foreign stadium singing John Denver classics, waving our nation's flag enthusiastically to cheer our athletes to gold, or simply engaging with strangers through the universal language of sport.

It has never been just a game. It is much more.

Acknowledgements

I OWE a special thanks to Gail Whitaker and Martie Whitaker. Without their kindness and extreme generosity, this book would not have been written. Martie first responded to my random direct message to her Twitter account in 2017. At the same time, I was contacting her stepsister, Gail, via a funeral service provider with a query about her father.

A few weeks later Gail happened to be in London with her granddaughter and she bought me a pizza while she shared stories about Denny. Fifteen months after our meal, Gail drove all the way from Florida to meet me in Burlington, Ontario to record an interview about her father and the Tea Bowl. At least I was able to return the favour and treated her to lunch and a ticket to the Hamilton Tiger-Cats.

Martie provided me with the material Denis Whitaker had been working on with her mother, Shelagh Whitaker. Denny and his wife had the idea for a book about the Tea Bowl. I had promised Martie that I would keep those notes safe until my work was finished. I recorded a documentary for the BBC about the game, but always wanted to do her stepfather and his team-mates justice. I have looked forward to the moment that I can return Denny and Shelagh's notes to her. Martie, I cannot thank you enough.

And Gail, your support and kindness will never be forgotten.

To Basil Russ's wonderful family, who gave up so much of their time to share his remarkable story. Gina Bower, Amelia Schulkins, Janice Kiner, Renee Hoffman.

Robert Arthur Grey Rowe, who generously provided me with a copy of the biography he wrote about his father, *Pappy*. It was a great source for my research.

Tom Slater gave up his time to drive me around Sarnia to educate me on Charles 'Hank' Living and Nick Paithouski. Tom's work on the *Sarnia War Remembrance Project* is nothing short of phenomenal.

Jason Horton from the BBC gave me the opportunity to initially bring this story to life. I remain grateful for the backing he gave me. And to Joel Hammer at the World Service who got my radio documentary on air.

Marc Sessler for trusting me after I approached him from the toilets in the Tottenham Hotspur Stadium's media café. He could have snubbed my unorthodox hand-written request, but instead he gave me his time for this project.

Thank you to the brilliant Claire Parnell from NFL UK who helped with my interview requests. Without her support there would be massive gaps in this book.

Oliver Luck for being a true gentleman. The hour we had over coffee in Frankfurt will be something I shall remember forever.

Dave McGinnis for sparing his time to share his memories of Pat Tillman. Those stories were tough for him to tell, and I remain indebted to his goodwill.

Peter King, who had better things to do than chat to me at the Kansas City Chiefs' press conference in Germany, but he dropped everything to do so.

Andrew Gamble, who kept telling me to 'write the book'. That beer in Phoenix definitely made this happen.

An honourable mention goes to my good friend Dave Oliver, who rekindled my affection for the NFL many moons ago. Your messages of support throughout this process were more motivating than you will know. And thanks to Ken Blanton, my North American 'brother' with whom I can forever talk ball.

To Matt Mackay, the most selfless person I know and a great friend whose shared interests in the war helped inspire my research. Time in your company is always lively and seemingly ageless.

My brother, Nick, your belief in me has been a constant source of inspiration.

Finally, the biggest thanks of all goes to my wife, Julia. Your belief and support have got me to this point. Thank you for your patience while I worked on this project. It has taken away much of our family time, even our summer holiday, but you remained loyal throughout. I could not have done this without you. There are times in the NFL season where you become a widow, but your understanding has been the catalyst for my success. One day we will watch a game together as a family, I promise.

Notes

AUTHOR INTERVIEWS

Steve Rains, Paul Vickers, Gail Whitaker Thompson, Mark Zuehlke, Sharon Early, Steve Daniel, Joe Horrigan, Peter Young, Mike Richman, Anne Madarasz, Richard Crepeau, Michael Bradley, Tom Slater, Janet Baker, Terry Millward, Roger Hart, Dave McGinnis, Gina Bower, Marc Sessler, Peter King, Oliver Luck, Henry Hodgson

CHAPTER 1: THE TOLL OF WAR

Paul Vickers quote, 'They did get a warm …'

'Disaster at Dieppe', CBC (2001)

Gail Thompson Whitaker, *A Soldier and Patriot: The Life of WM Denis Whitaker – Tragedy at Dieppe*, by Mark Zuehlke

Schick, Joshua, *Operation Jubilee: The Raid at Dieppe* (The National World War II Museum, October 2021)

The National World War II Museum

The Incredible Story of the Dambuster Raid 1943, Imperial War Museum

Tips for American Servicemen in Britain During the Second World War, Imperial War Museum

Denis Whitaker quote, 'I started talking to a fellow next to me …' from manuscript 'The Game That Stopped the War', by Denis and Shelagh Whitaker

CHAPTER 2: DENIS WHITAKER: A WARRIOR THAT WAS GREAT

'Denis Whitaker, 86, Highly Decorated Canadian War Hero', the *New York Times*, June 9, 2001

Battle of Goch-Calcar Road, Gail Thompson Whitaker, *A Soldier and Patriot: The Life of WM Denis Whitaker – Tragedy at Dieppe*, by Mark Zuehlke

Royal Military College of Canada

International Churchill Society

'We Were Sitting Ducks': 100-year-old veteran shares Dieppe raid memories, by Morgan Lowrie, the *Canadian Press*

CHAPTER 3: CANADIAN FOOTBALL'S EXODUS

CFL Hall of Fame

Steve Daniel quote, 'Canadian Football in those days …'; 'In those days …'

Gail Whitaker Thompson quote, 'At that time in the war …'; 'They were waiting, waiting, waiting …'

CHAPTER 4: PEARL HARBOR

Joe Horrigan quote, 'News was trickling out …'; 'indications were happening …'; 'obviously, we knew …'

Chicago Tribune 'Flashback update: Bears game on Dec. 7, 1941'

Pro Football Reference

New York Daily News

Washington Post

Mike Richman, commanders.com

CHAPTER 5: NFL CARRIES ON

Pro Football Hall of Fame

Green Bay Packers

Washington Post

Mike Richman, commanders.com

CHAPTER 6: THE STEAGLES

The Steagles: An Unforgettable 1943 Season, by Ray Dindinger, philadelphiaeagles.com, November 8, 2018

Joe Horrigan quote, 'One player once put it ...'

CHAPTER 7: AMERICAN FOOTBALL ON FOREIGN FIELDS

'Hale vs. Yarvard at Ravenhill Stadium, Belfast', Wartime NI

Ireland's Saturday Night (14 November 1942)

8,000 Irish Fans Puzzled by US Football Game, *Stars and Stripes*, November 16, 1942

'Service elevens evenly matched for grid game', *Star and Stripes* (May 7, 1943)

'Crimson Tide Eleven Rolls Fighting Irish, 19-6', *Stars and Stripes* (May 10, 1943)

Harrisburg Telegraph, July 22, 1943

'Football! Navy! War! How Military "Lend-Lease" Players Saved the College Game and Helped Win World War II', by Wilbur D. Jones Jnr.

'It was also the case in boxing matches and wrestling matches,' Richard Crepeau, Professor Emeritus of History at University of Central Florida, Orlando

Society for American Baseball Research

'Present more individual stars than even the World Series on the mainland ... a titanic battle between some of the best-known players in baseball', Gayle Hayes from the *Honolulu Advertiser*

CHAPTER 8: ALL-STAR LINE-UP

Riders Ready for Saturday's Final, *Winnipeg Tribune*, November 27, 1941

Fraser Bemoans Placement, *Winnipeg Tribune*, December 1, 1941

Ottawa Citizen, September 4, 1941

Capt. Orville Burke Helps to Stop Germans Rushing East to Ems River, by Douglas Amaron, *Ottawa Citizen*, April 12, 1945

Orville Burke Lost to Rough Riders, by Tommy Shields, *Ottawa Citizen*, September 5, 1946

Sir Edwin Leather: Forceful Conservative politician, *The Independent*, April 9, 2005

Sir Edwin Leather obituary, *The Telegraph*, April 6, 2005

bluebombers.com

CFL Hall of Fame

Ottawa Forwards Badly Outplayed as Bombers Win, The *Winnipeg Tribune*, December 11, 1939

Andy Bieber obituary, *Winnipeg Free Press*, November 19, 1985

Argos Mourn the Loss of Ken Turnbull, September 16, 2008

Kenneth Turnbull Obituary

The Suez Crisis, 1956: United States Office of the Historian

CHAPTER 9: JEFF NICKLIN

Steve Daniel quote, 'What I would say about Jeff Nicklin is that he …'

Bernd Horn, 'Bradbrooke, Nicklin and Eadie – A Tale of Command,' in Colonel Bernd Horn, ed., *Intrepid Warriors. Perspectives on Canadian Military Leaders* (Toronto: Dundurn Group, 2007), 223–260

'Nicklin's Death in Action Blow to Sport in Canada' – Maurice Smith, *Winnipeg Free Press*, 1945

'Lest We Forget – The Jeff Nicklin Story' by Ed Tait, Winnipeg Blue Bombers

'Jeff Nicklin's Lucky Escape' – Russ Munro, *Winnipeg Tribune*, 1945

'Helpless After 'Chute Leap Jeff Nicklin Slain by Foe' – Frederick Griffin, *Toronto Star*, March 1945

'Canada should embrace our heroes, not forget them' – Jerry Amernic, *The Hub*, March 24, 2022

CHAPTER 10: TOMMY THOMPSON

Joe Horrigan quote 'Tommy Thompson kind of was that ultimate throwback player ...'

Sharon Early quote 'You know, the story goes that he was probably around eight years old ...'

Eagles Great Tommy Thompson Finally Makes Phila. Sport Hall of Fame, by Frank Fitzpatrick, *The Philadelphia Inquirer*, November 8, 2012

Pro Football Hall of Fame; Earle Neale

'Win, Lose or Draw', Bernard Hawkins, *Washington Evening Star*, December 20, 1948

'Eagles Bury Rams' Crown Hopes, 14-0', *Berkeley Daily Gazette*, December 19, 1949

CHAPTER 11: PAUL 'PAPPY' ROWE

Stamps Legacy: Paul Rowe, by Bill Powers, Stampeders.com, October 19, 2010

Pappy: The Life Story of Hall of Fame Great Paul Rowe, by Robert Arthur Grey Rowe

Steve Daniel quote, 'Paul Rowe was immediately one of the stars of the league in 1938 …'

All Blacks website: stats.allblacks.com

Time Out with Maurice Smith: *Winnipeg Free Press*, November 12, 1948

The 'Sleeper Play,' staples in the Big O, the 13th man and the Fog Bowl: 105 years of Grey Cup classics, by Stephen Hunt, November 23, 2018, CBC News

Greatest Grey Cup Champion: 1948 Calgary Stampeders, by Matthew Scianitti, November 17, 2020, TSN

CHAPTER 12: THE SMALL TOWN WITH BIG HEROES

Michael Bradley quote, 'We're not an old city …'

Sarnia Imperials – The Last Amateur Grey Cup Champions, 13th Man Sports

Lambton Heritage Museum

Sarnia Lambton Sports Hall of Fame

The Sarnia War Remembrance Project by Tom Slater

Queen's University: The Paithouski Prize

Queen's University Athletics and Recreation: gogaels.com

Janet Baker quote, 'Basically, he was designing and …'

The RCAF at War, by Frank Phripp

CHAPTER 13: BASIL F. RUSS

Gina Bower quote, 'He did not want to …'

CHAPTER 14: THE RIGHT HONOURABLE GEORGE HEES

'Riders Ready for Saturday's Final', *Winnipeg Tribune*, November 27, 1941

The Canadian Encyclopaedia: George Harris Hees (Obituary)

Government of Canada: The Honourable George Hees 1910–1996 (Posthumous)

Government of Canada: George Hees Fonds

The Brandon Sun, June 13, 1996, 'World War II veteran and ex-cabinet minister Hees dead at 85', by John Ward of the Canadian Press

Rare Courage, Veterans of the Second World War Remember, by Rod Mickleburgh, published by McCelland & Stewart in 2005Canadiansoldiers.com – Walcheren Causeway

Debates of June 17th, 1996, Open Parliament, Canada

'Mr Hees was a great sportsman …' MP Louis Plamondon

'George's service to his country was automatic …' Deborah Grey

'I had the opportunity to sit in the House of Commons with Mr Hees for nine years …' Bill Blaikie

CHAPTER 15: CHEERS TO FOOTBALL

Denis Whitaker quote, 'It really was an All-Star …'

Stars and Stripes, Gene Graff, February 4, 1944

CHAPTER 16: THE TEA BOWL, FEBRUARY 13, 1944

Denis Whitaker quote, 'I guess we were in a minority …' courtesy of Shelagh Whitaker, Martie Whitaker and the Whitaker family

The Game That Stopped the War, as told by W. Denis Whitaker, 1996

Memorandum for broadcast details by Karl Hoffenberg, Program Director, February 1, 1944. Memorandum courtesy of BBC Written Archives

Canucks to Battle Yanks in 'Tea Bowl,' the *Lethbridge Herald*, February 1, 1944

Ken Turnbull quote, 'The *esprit de corps* was terrific ...'

The Canucks Take Yanks, by Allan Nickleson, the *Canadian Press News*, February 19, 1944

Stars and Stripes, February 14, 1944

Canadian Army Wins Tea Bowl, Associated Press, February 13, 1944

Lt. Orville Burk Dominates "Tea Bowl" Game In London, *Canadian Press*, February 13, 1944

Canadian–American Army Rugby Game: Sportscast by Capt. Ted Leather, February 14, 1944

CHAPTER 17: THE COFFEE BOWL, MARCH 19, 1944

Ken Turnbull quote, 'In the second game...' courtesy of Martie Whitaker and Whitaker family

Player quote, 'I came face to face with this guy ...' courtesy of Martie Whitaker and Whitaker family

Stars and Stripes, March 20, 1944, 'Blues Blank Canadians, 18-0,' by Gene Graff

Medicine Hat Daily News, March 21, 1944, 'Britishers Baffled,' by Allan Nickleson

Winnipeg Tribune, March 20, 1944, 'Coffee Bowl Comeback'

CHAPTER 18: PLAYERS LOST

Pro Football Hall of Fame

Joe Horrigan quote, 'There were stellar performances on the field ...'

Congressional Medal of Honor Society

National World War II Museum in New Orleans

CHAPTER 19: WARTIME RIVALRY

Mike Richman, author of *The Redskins Encyclopaedia*

Larry Mayer, Chicago Bears senior writer

Pro Football Hall of Fame

Jewish Virtual Library

The Steagles: An Unforgettable 1943 Season, by Ray Dindinger, philadelphiaeagles.com, November 8, 2018

CHAPTER 20: THE UNITED SERVICE ORGANIZATIONS

The United Service Organizations, uso.org

Marc Sessler quote

Oliver Luck quote

CHAPTER 21: THE NFL AND THE ARMED FORCES

Paul Tagliabue quote, 'We've become the winter version of the Fourth of July celebration.' From 1991 State-of-the-League news conference

Nfl.com Salute to Service

George Kittle quote, 'Every time I get a …'

Let's Go! with Tom Brady, Larry Fitzgerald and Jim Gray, by SiriusXM, October 22, 2022

Jaelen Phillips quote, 'Oh, I think it's super important …'

Peter King quote, 'I think a lot of it has to do …'

Oliver Luck quote, 'Whether it's the UK or Germany …'

The Civil Rights Struggle, African-American GIs, and Germany: aacvr-germany.org

CHAPTER 22: PAT TILLMAN

Dave McGinnis quote, 'We just loved him …'

Pat's Story, the Pat Tillman Foundation

Shooter Fears He Killed Pat Tillman, by Mike Fisher for ESPN, April 16, 2014

CHAPTER 23: A TEAM IS BORN

'For me it kicked off,' Terry Millward

'The NFL was something different,' Roger Hart

'Salazar, Rojas served country, now serve Granite', Michael Lingberg, *The Porterville Recorder,* February 3, 2014

'Top UK Soccer Executive: London NFL team "only a matter of time",' Glenn Price, April 12, 2014, americanfootballinternational.com

CHAPTER 24: THE GROWTH OF AMERICAN FOOTBALL

Oliver Luck quote, 'So, Pete Rozelle's tenure …'

Hey world, welcome to American Football, by Barry Wilner, Associated Press, March 23, 1991

Doubts running high as WLAF prepares for openers, Associated Press, March 23, 1991

The NFL's First Real Foray Overseas, 30 Years Later, by Alex Prewitt for *Sports Illustrated*

The NFL in Germany, an oral history: 'Beer and brats. It's like being in Wisconsin' by Greg Auman for The Athletic, Nov 11, 2022

CHAPTER 25: THE NEXT STEP

NFL statement: 'Tottenham Hotspur and NFL Announce Expanded Partnership Through 2029–2030 Season', September 14, 2023

Henry Hodgson quote, 'Alistair and I worked on …'

Giants beat Miami at wet Wembley – BBC Sport, October 28, 2007

Oliver Luck quote, 'I'm not sure we …'

Peter King quote, 'Until a few years ago …'

Shahid Khan quote, 'It's a win-win-win …'

Tom Brady quote, 'That was one of the great football …'

John Harbaugh quote, 'I don't plan on going …'

John Harbaugh quote, 'It's a great feeling …'

Danny Crossman quote, 'I think it's fabulous …'

Frank Smith quote, 'It's been great …'

Raheem Mostert quote, 'Yeah, it's been fairly …'

Bradley Chubb quote, 'The sky's the limit …'

'The NFL Academy Announces Three Games Against Renowned US High Schools This Fall', NFL statement, August 2, 2023

'Global American Football Family Reacts to Confirmation of Flag Football's Inclusion in the Olympic Games Los Angeles 2028', NFL statement, October 16, 2023

'Olympic Truce', from the International Olympic Committee website, Olympics.com